Big Body Play

Why Boisterous, Vigorous, and Very Physical Play Is
Essential to Children's Development and Learning

Frances M. Carlson

National Association for the Education of Young Children
Washington, DC

National Association for the
Education of Young Children
1313 L Street NW, Suite 500
Washington, DC 20005-4101
202-232-8777 • 800-424-2460
www.naeyc.org

NAEYC Books

Editor in Chief
Akimi Gibson

Editorial Director
Bry Pollack

Senior Editor
Holly Bohart

Design and Production
Malini Dominey

Assistant Editor
Elizabeth Wegner

Editorial Assistant
Ryan Smith

Permissions
Lacy Thompson

Through its publications program, the National Association for the Education of Young Children (NAEYC) provides a forum for discussion of major issues and ideas in the early childhood field, with the hope of provoking thought and promoting professional growth. The views expressed or implied in this book are not necessarily those of the Association or its members.

Permissions

NASPE Guidelines for Physical Activity (chart, p. 25) reprinted from *Active Start: A Statement of Physical Activity Guidelines for Children From Birth to Age 5, 2nd ed.,* and *Physical Activity for Children (5-12),* with permission from the National Association for Sport and Physical Education (NASPE), 1900 Association Drive, Reston, VA 20191, www.NASPEinfo.org.

Photo Credits

Copyright © by: Rebecca Anlas: 22. Bonnie Blagojevic: 71. Natalie Bennett: cover (second from bottom), i (left), 2, 8 (left), 12, 38, 44, 61 (bottom), 92-93, back cover (top). Carly Brown: 18. Caty Carlson: v. Frances Carlson: 48, 60, 61 (top and middle). Brand X Pictures: cover (bottom). Donna Danoff: 20. Malini Dominey: 74. Tyler Hamlet: 94. Higher Horizons: 63. Julia Luckenbill: cover (third from top), 56. Sherie W. Mescher: 9 (left). Marilyn Nolt: 9 (right), 35. Ellen B. Senisi: cover (top and second from top), i (middle and right), vi, viii, 4, 8 (right), 52, 66, back cover (middle and bottom). Deb Wittkowski: 80.

Copyright © NAEYC: Peg Callaghan: 26, 27. Mary and Steve Skjold: 10. Susan Woog Wagner: 15, 30, 43.

Thanks to BrightLIFE, A Kid's Campus at Life University (http://centers.brighthorizons.com/brightlife) for the outdoor playscape location: 60-61.

Contributing editor: *Heather Biggar Tomlinson*
Editorial assistance: *Melissa Hogarty*

Big Body Play: Why Boisterous, Vigorous, and Very Physical Play Is Essential to Children's Development and Learning

Library of Congress Control Number: 2011926727
ISBN: 978-1-928896-71-5

NAEYC Item #241

To Alexander, Jon, Adam, Sam, and Caty . . .
and Sunday afternoons playing Team at Grandma's house.

Acknowledgments

Next to raising my three children, writing books is the most difficult undertaking I've ever attempted. And, as with raising children, I'm so thankful I don't have to do it alone. I'd like to thank the following people for supporting me in this book's journey: To my family, thank you for always being the best part of my day every day. Thanks to my students at Chattahoochee Technical College and Mercer University, as well as participants at conferences where I've presented—especially the Manitoba Child Care Association annual conferences—for caring about this topic and for being so candid with your opinions and experiences. I am privileged to have worked with each one of you.

Thank you to my colleagues at Chattahoochee Technical College for being passionate about young children, and for letting me run so many of my ideas by you for feedback and perspective; to Rick Porter for bringing attention to this important play more than 20 years ago; to Marcy Smith for being Marcy Smith; to Bryan Nelson for letting me talk through every chapter while we walked Winnipeg because that's when it all began to make sense; to MenTeach–New England for being available 24/7 to assist me in so many, many ways—thanks, guys . . . y'all are the best!

Thank you to Norma Luster and the infant classroom teachers, families, and children at The Children's Center at All Saints' in Atlanta, Georgia, for letting me observe and photograph; to Rebecca Koch, Susan Holliday, Teresa Orefice, and Bright LIFE, A Kid's Campus at Life University in Marietta, Georgia, for allowing me to spotlight their natural outdoor playscape and the wonderful way it supports big body play; to Natalie Bennett for being my photography, shopping, sushi, and coffee buddy; and especially to Ron Blatz for opening my eyes to the importance of this topic and for supporting my work in and about it. Special thanks to Akimi Gibson for her vision and clarity, to Bry Pollack for her unwavering belief in this book and in me, and to Holly Bohart for helping me with the last, crucial steps.

About the Author

 **Frances Carlson** teaches early childhood education in an associate degree program at Chattahoochee Technical College. Carlson has worked as center administrator for child care programs in Oklahoma and for the Department of the Army in Italy, the Sheltering Arms, Internal Revenue Service, Wachovia Bank, Turner Broadcasting Systems, and the child development lab school at Chattahoochee Technical College. She has led four child care programs successfully through the NAEYC Accreditation process.

Frances has a bachelor's degree in English from North Georgia College & State University, a certificate in Italian from the Defense Language Institute/Foreign Language Center at the Presidio of Monterey, and a master's degree in education from Concordia University–St. Paul.

Frances authored the NAEYC book *Essential Touch: Meeting the Needs of Young Children* (2006) and directed and produced the DVD *Expect Male Involvement: Recruiting & Retaining Men in ECE* (2009).

In her free time, Frances enjoys riding her bike, cooking for her family and friends, and going to movies.

Contents

How I Came to Write This Book . . . and Why It Is Needed

Young children play vigorously, boisterously, and even roughly with their and with other children's bodies. Like most adults, I have often questioned whether I should stop this rough style of play for fear a child will get hurt, or whether I should allow it because I remember playing this way as a child. Let me tell you how I have come to believe strongly that, when properly supervised, children's big body play can and should be an integral part of early childhood settings.

While participating in the Working Forum on Men in Early Childhood Education in 2008, I attended a session in which Ron Blatz, executive director of the Children's Discovery Centre in Winnipeg, Manitoba, Canada, spoke about gender perspectives among adults and how these perspectives affect children's care. He told a story about how some of his male teachers had supervised the children on the playground as they took turns jumping on the end of a board to flip items off the other end. The play was rowdy, risk-taking, and very physical. Ron commented that both teachers and children had benefited from the experience but that if the female teachers had been supervising it, the children would have never been allowed to have this experience.

I was outraged! How dare he suggest that female teachers have no appreciation for children's rowdy physical play and that they focus too much on safety? Who did he think he was?

When I returned home I related Ron's story and its negative effect on me to my husband, who promptly burst out laughing. I was shocked. "Why are you laughing?" I asked him. He said, "Because he's right! Don't you

remember all the times the kids would be on the trampoline and you would tell them to stop whatever they were doing 'before someone gets hurt'?"

He was right. Even though I was introduced to the concept that children's rough play was beneficial when I was researching my book *Essential Touch*, I had failed to integrate that learning into my actual practice. I knew rough play was important for young children, but I didn't know why all children seemed to gravitate toward it or how to encourage it. I realized Ron had just taught me a very important lesson: Without understanding why rough play is necessary for young children's development and that its risks can be managed, teachers—especially female teachers—are likely to shut it down to protect the children in their care.

I believe in evidence-based practice, so I knew that before I could fully integrate the idea that rough-and-tumble play is good for children, I had to know more. I had to know what the research said about this play style and the benefits it offers. I had to know about others' experiences with rough play. I had to spend some time reflecting on what my own common sense said about children's need to take risks and our need as teachers and supervisors to protect and safeguard them. So that's what I did. I read volumes of research from the field. I spoke to hundreds of teachers around the country and the world. I talked to my friends and my own children.

I also spent some time reminiscing about my best childhood memories, the times my sister flew me around in the living room on her upraised legs, and the times my brother and I took turns jumping off the doghouse or jumping back and forth between the beds. I also remembered all the Sunday afternoons my children spent in the backyard at their grandma's house playing a game they called "Team" with their cousins. The play was loud, rowdy, and very physical. Those Sunday afternoons playing Team are among their favorite childhood memories.

Three years later, I now know and understand the fundamental need young children have to both experiment with and learn from their bodies in such a physical way. I know why this play aids their overall development, as well as how we—teachers, administrators, trainers, professors, policy makers, and families—can provide for and supervise it so that children can garner optimum benefits with minimal risk to their safety.

About this book

Chapter 1 defines *big body play*, examines common misunderstandings about it, and explains how it differs from aggression. Chapter 2 provides information about how big body play affects every part of a child's healthy development. Chapter 3 shows how to understand the importance of risk in learning and how to plan environments, policies, and supervision to best support this play style without endangering children.

We know that to develop to their full potential, children need to experience appropriate risks and challenges. Acknowledging both the contributions and the risks of rough-and-tumble play allows us to plan for it and supervise it intentionally and enthusiastically. If you have ever voiced, or heard voiced, a concern about children's rough-and-tumble play, this book is for you.

Chapter 1

What Is "Big Body Play"?

Our kids love to roll. It seems like wherever we go, winter or summer, they find hills to roll down. Sometimes they roll head over heels, sometimes sideways, sometimes alone, but more often in groups. I have lots of memories of large masses of children, different shapes and sizes, just letting themselves go down snowy or grassy hills, usually rolling and tumbling over each other.

—An after-school coordinator

Rolling, running, climbing, chasing, pushing, banging, tagging, falling, tumbling, rough-and-tumble, rowdy, roughhousing, horseplay, play-fighting. These are just some of the names that adults give to the boisterous, large motor, very physical activity that young children naturally seem to crave. All are forms of *big body play*—a play style that gives children the opportunities they need for optimum development across all domains from physical to cognitive and language to social and emotional.

Types of big body play

From birth, children use their bodies to learn. As infants, they roll back and forth, kick their legs, and wave their arms. As toddlers, they pull each other, hug each other tightly, and push each other down. In the preschool years and beyond, these very physical ways of interacting and learning become even more rowdy as well as complex and social.

Humans are not the only animals that play in this boisterous, physical way. Puppies wrestle, drag each other around, run, and tussle. Kittens roll and tumble, chase, and pounce. In all animals studied at play—humans

5

included—males engage in rough-and-tumble play more than females do (Pellegrini & Smith 1998b; Power 2000). In fact, boys are more physically active overall than girls are (Finn et al. 2002). (See "Rough-and-Tumble Play for Boys" in chapter 2.)

Children engage in big body play in many different ways: alone, with others, with objects, in rough-and-tumble fashion, and in organized games with rules. For example, they may play alone or alongside another in an activity that is very vigorous and poses a physical challenge—running around, dancing and swirling, rolling on the floor, hopping and skipping along.

A toddler teacher shared this experience of her children's play:

> We have a big, comfy loveseat in the reading area of the classroom. One of my children's favorite things to do is have me toss them onto the loveseat. They laugh, roll off, and then come back so I can toss them again. A couple of them would rather spend 5 or so minutes being tossed than doing anything else in the classroom. It's great fun—for me and them—and it reminds me why I love being an early childhood teacher!

Sometimes children incorporate objects into their big body play. Slides and mounted playground structures are favorite bases for children to climb up before flinging themselves to the ground below. Children may use large yoga balls and roll their bodies on them. Sometimes they pedal their tricycles into mounted structures or into fences. They will climb the slide to get to the top of the structure, instead of walking up the stairs, and then slide back down.

Most often, for older children, big body play includes body contact between children (and sometimes between children and adult) in *rough-and-tumble play* or in organized games. In rough-and-tumble play we see them wrestle each other to the ground, swing each other around, chase and tag each other, and crawl on top of each other. Children will sometimes wrap their arms around each other and then roll—down a hill, across a yard, or into a fence. Sometimes children use their legs and feet in pretend fighting, or *play-fighting*.

Children play this way most often with others they consider as friends, and generally children enjoy it (Schafer & Smith 1996). They may invite others to simply tag and flee, flee and chase, grab and roll, run and grab, or lunge at each other with open palms. Such play is often the result of a friend saying to another friend, "Hey! Let's run to the fence. First one there wins!"

When playing in these rowdy and boisterous ways, children exhibit several signs of enjoying the play: They smile and laugh, join the activity voluntarily, and readily return for more, time and time again. Their faces are free and easy, and their muscle tone is relaxed. Here's an example in which the children have chosen the activity willingly, they are playing co-operatively together, and their play is accompanied by laughter:

> Three children in the preK classroom are outside on the playground. They stand close, each one behind the next, like cars in a train. The two in the rear place their hands flat on the back of the child in front of them . . . then they push! All the kids fall down. They all get up, turn to face in the opposite direction, and repeat the whole process, over and over for 15 or 20 minutes, laughing the whole time.

Sometimes young children play more traditional body games with an accepted set of rules. For example, they may choose one child to be "It" while the others run around. The rules are that whoever is It has to tag another child; the tagged child then becomes It. These rules are usually accepted and understood by the children at the play's onset.

At other times, children make up impromptu games with their own rules. A mother of three children recalled:

> The kids loved to go outside and get on the trampoline. One of them would lie in the center while the other two ran around the edge, hopping and jumping as the one in the middle bounced around. They had a rule that the one in the middle had to stay in the middle and couldn't try to stand up while the others were running. Our rule was that the running ones had to stay at the edge and away from the one in the middle.

Teachers and children together may make up rough-and-tumble games:

> My favorite rough-and-tumble play is when we make a "grilled cheese sandwich." One child lies faceup on a mat (bread). Another child lies down on top of that child (cheese) and then another child lies down on top (bread). Then I'll say, "Oh, no! It's time to flip the sandwich!" All three kids tip over, and then we start over again, and again, and again!

Why big body play is essential

We know that play such as sociodramatic play, board games, play to explore objects and learn shapes and textures, finger plays and chants to improve self-regulation, and play that involves building things has myriad benefits for children. But the fleeing, tagging, climbing, tumbling, and wrestling that most young children seem to crave is also play and is equally beneficial.

As we might assume, there are abundant positive effects for physical development when children are active in their play. We know, for example, that when teachers involve children in physical exercise with intentional planning, children can practice and develop a variety of physical skills and gain optimum health benefits (Sanders 2002).

With the value that rough-and-tumble play has for physical and social development, we should work it in as a center and allow the children to engage in it like they would other classroom centers, such as blocks, reading, or puzzles.

—ECE college student

Continuum of Young Children's Physical Development

We generally do not describe young children's very physical activity as "rough-and-tumble play" or "roughhousing" or "play-fighting" until they become preschoolers. But the vigorous physical movement and forceful body contact that are characteristic of big body play are part of children's life experience right from the start.

As newborns grow into toddlers, then into preschoolers and primary-grade students, physical maturity and activity typically follow a clear progression. Understanding children's physical development at all stages will help adults strike a balance between keeping children safe and enabling them to take appropriate risks.

Infants

Before birth, the growing fetus twists, turns, kicks, and shoves its mother (and occasionally its in utero sibling) from the inside. At the same time, the baby constantly is being jostled in the amniotic sac as the mother moves about. Then the process of labor and delivery squeezes and rolls the newborn's body.

From their first months, infants engage in forms of big body play. They grab their feet, roll side to side, kick, wave, and scoot on their bellies or backs. Infants at 6 months old spend as much as 40 percent of an hour of playtime in this body-rocking and foot-kicking activity (Pellegrini & Smith 1998a). Much of the time, the infant's physical play is solitary; but when two infants are in close enough proximity to each other, they may engage each other by grabbing and squeezing each other's hands, arms, feet, and legs and by rolling on top of each other.

Caregivers often engage an infant in many types of vigorous body play, as well. Around the world, adults bounce babies on their knees (playing "horsey"); hold babies in upraised arms to fly through the air; drop them from a close distance onto a soft mattress, bean bag, or big pile of warm laundry; or gently toss and catch them. Because infants typically smile, squeal, laugh, and gurgle when played with this way, we adults tend to perform these actions over and over again.

As much as infants enjoy this adult-led big body play, though, most often infants engage in their physical play without an adult's participation (Pellegrini & Smith 1998a).

Toddlers

Once a child learns to walk, an explosion of movement occurs and gross motor skills advance exponentially. Toddlers quickly attempt and master (or almost master) big body play such as jumping, pushing, kicking a ball, tiptoeing, splashing through puddles, carrying armfuls of objects from place to place, running, and even pedaling.

Body awareness is a distinct component of self-awareness that develops from about 24 to 30 months (Brownell et al. 2007). However, because they are learning how to monitor their bodies in space, and because they are growing quite rapidly, toddlers' kinesthetic awareness rarely keeps pace with their actual physical growth and development. Consequently, they can take lots of tumbles as they misjudge distances or relative weight or strength. They have to continuously retest and relearn to keep up with the rapid changes happening to their bodies.

During the toddler years, there tends to be a considerable amount of parallel play, where children play side by side, sometimes copying each other, sometimes doing their own thing, and occasionally frolicking together—by rolling on each other, holding hands as they run, climbing on each other, or trying to simultaneously climb on the same tricycle, dog, or parent.

Preschoolers

A fundamental movement phase occurs between 2 and 7 years old, wherein coordination improves every year, making it an ideal time for adults to capitalize on development of children's basic physical skills such as running, throwing, and balancing (Gabbard 2007; Gal-

lahue 1995). At ages 2 and 3, children are still quite uncoordinated, but by 4 and 5 years old, although still a little clumsy, they have more control over their movements. By preschool age, children spend five percent of their free time in big body play (Pellegrini 1987).

Kindergartners

By kindergarten, children are captivated by discovering what their bodies can do, determining how high they can climb, how far they can jump, how fast they can run, how well they can pedal, and so forth. They have better balance than before, longer, leaner bodies, and an improved social ability to cooperate with peers (Thelen & Smith 1998), which is essential for successful interactive rough-and-tumble play. They can participate in games with reciprocal roles and tend to be intensely interested in getting along and forming friendships (McClelland et al. 2006).

In addition to the social changes, kindergartners' bodies are ready for the more careful and calibrated physicality of safe rough-and-tumble play. They can run and change directions smoothly, can shift weight well and vary the force of their body, and are more able to "give" with their body to absorb force (Robertson 1984).

(continued)

Early primary grades

Between 6 and 8 years of age, children become even more fluid in how they move (Sanders 2006). By age 7, the time spent in rough-and-tumble play doubles, to about 13 percent (Pellegrini 1987).

By this age, children usually experience good health and fewer illnesses, and physical growth is a bit less rapid, in spite of occasional growth spurts (Starfield 1994). Muscle mass increases in both boys and girls, but skeletal and ligament development is not by any means complete or mature.

Although gross motor skills such as running and jumping are already established before the primary grades, children refine these skills even further and become more purposeful and controlled in their movements. They have better coordination and balance and greater endurance, as well. They have good use of all their various body parts. In addition, they are more aware of their body's position and movements.

Children in the early primary grades are delighted by their increasingly honed physical skills and thrive on independence and risk taking. These changes result in greater abilities related to rough-and-tumble play, as children become even more interested in the physical and social engagement that wrestling, tackling, and chasing provide. In particular, they are intrigued by determining relative physical strengths and weaknesses between themselves and their peers—they ask themselves, who can use the monkey swings longer, who is heavier, who is faster in a race, who is better able to catch a ball, who has better balance on a bike?

They are somewhat more at risk of harm in rough play because of their penchant for risk taking, their incomplete knowledge of their limits, and their incomplete bone and ligament development.

—Heather Biggar Tomlinson

But big body play is not just physical activity with physical benefits. During such play, children also use increasingly sophisticated communication skills—both verbal and nonverbal—and social skills. It is also one of the best ways for children (especially boys) to develop empathy and self-regulation. And creativity and thinking skills are enhanced as children determine and solve problems as they arise in the course of this active play. For example,

> Several preschoolers are playing a game of Tag. Several children race to the opposite end of the playground to avoid being tagged. Some of the others voice concerns that these children have run too far away to be caught, so they discuss the problem and decide to set the closest two outside fences as boundaries. The play resumes and continues without interruption for 20 minutes.

Big body play provides children the varied opportunities they need to thrive physically, socially, emotionally, and cognitively. Chapter 2 will provide an in-depth look at the wide-ranging benefits this exuberant play offers children.

Reservations and misunderstandings about big body play

Most adults can remember running, wrestling, rolling, and roughhousing as children with their friends and siblings, and loving to play this way. For a variety of reasons, however, this rowdy, vigorous style of play is not valued much today. The intense focus on academics, and especially on including technology in each classroom, has left funding for physical education at an all-time low (DeCorby et al. 2005). Physical activity as a whole is undervalued, especially in the early primary grades.

Another reason may be that Western society in general, and the workplace in particular, seems to be shifting away from an appreciation for such traditionally male characteristics as physical prowess, dominance, and quick decision making and toward an emphasis on traditionally female traits of self-control and strong communication skills (Rosin 2010). Less physical traits—social intelligence, open communication, and the ability to sit still and focus—are seen as more valuable in today's economy, and this viewpoint may be finding its way into early education.

In early childhood settings, too many adults who work with young children doubt the validity and appropriateness—much less the developmental *necessity*—of this boisterous and very physical play style. Some tolerate it. Some discount it. Most accept that all children have the impulse to

A favorite childhood memory of one elderly woman who had been a preschool teacher is jumping off hay bales into snow drifts.

engage in it. But as rich and varied as the benefits of such play are, almost all adults admit to stopping or banning at least its rough-and-tumble forms. This is generally motivated by of one or more of the following fears.

Fear of fighting

The fear of children fighting and injuring themselves or others is not entirely misplaced. *Fighting*—defined as physical acts used to coerce or control another person, through either inflicting pain or the threat of pain—does occur. Here's an example from a teacher of 3- and 4-year-olds:

> I was outside with my young preschool class. Suddenly one child walked over to a second child and, using his open hand, struck the second child on the side of his head. Before I could act, the second child reached up with a closed fist and hit the first child three or four times on the side of his head. Both children burst into tears and ran away.

Many people think that when children are engaged in rough-and-tumble play, they are actually fighting. They are not. Such play, by definition, does not involve acts of real fighting (Schafer & Smith 1996). (More on this key point in the section "The Myth That Rough-and-Tumble Play Is Aggression.") Consider the following vignette, in which the teacher mistakes play for fighting:

> I was in my preK classroom late in the afternoon; only five or six children were still there. Two of the boys went to the block center rug to wrestle. They were really going at it—scuffling and rolling around with their arms tightly around each other. I watched them to make sure they were okay, and since they were smiling and laughing, I didn't stop them. Then my co-teacher came into the room, and she immediately went over to the boys and made them stop. She then chastised me for letting the kids "fight."

Although many teachers struggle to differentiate rough-and-tumble play from fighting, and overestimate the amount of real fighting that occurs during this play (Schafer & Smith 1996), young children easily distinguish between the two (Boulton 1993; Logue & Harvey 2009; Pellegrini 2002; Schafer & Smith 1996; Smith et al. 2002; 2004). When asked whether their rough-and-tumble play is fighting, young children are very clear: "We're playing, not fighting" . . . "It looks like I'm hitting him, but I'm not."

Fear of escalation

Some adults fear that even if children's rough-and-tumble play seems to be appropriate—the participants are enjoying it, and no one is getting hurt—it will inevitably lead to real fighting if allowed to continue. The prevailing body of research, however, supports the notion that rough-and-tumble play, although it may look aggressive, rarely leads to true aggression (DiPietro 1981; Fry 1990; 2005; Hellendoorn & Harinck 1997; Humphreys & Smith 1987; Paquette et al. 2003; Smith et al. 2004).

Why not? Because it is truly aggressive acts among young children, not play, that generally lead to more aggressive acts (Malloy & McMurray-Schwarz 2004).

The following is a teacher's example of children engaging in rough play without becoming aggressive:

> I supervise wrestling in my classroom. We set rules, such as no shoes allowed and the kids have to stay on the mat. They are very focused, and the wrestling lasts for two or three minutes. Then they get up, shake hands, and are relatively calm when they leave the mat, often smiling victoriously. Although the kids sometimes get frustrated, neither seems upset with the other when they are done.

Moreover, although preschool-age children spend roughly 10 percent of their outdoor free time engaged in big body play, their rough-and-tumble play leads to true fighting less than 1 percent of the time (Smith et al. 2004). When this does happen, it is generally because one child has mis-read another's social cue. This is an issue in particular with children whose lagging social skills prevent them from forming successful relationships (see the box "Socially Rejected or Awkward Children" in chapter 2). Such children have difficulty understanding cues and so turn friendly play into fighting much more often than do children whose social skills are developing typically (Smith et al. 2004).

Fear of agitation

Some adults believe that big body play riles kids up. Teachers may fear that once children get loud and rowdy during play, helping them to return to a calmer state for other activities will be challenging, if not altogether impossible, to do.

Although the initial physical activity is invigorating for children, the time period following their big body play finds them calmer and more focused than if they had lacked the chance to be so rowdy and boisterous (Scott & Panksepp 2003). Teachers must reflect on whether a child's loud, rowdy behavior is fundamentally inappropriate or simply irritating to the supervising adult.

Fear of injury

What parents and teachers seem to fear most about children's big body play is that children may get hurt. For example,

> Two boys are climbing up the slide. The lower boy reaches up and grabs the lead boy, putting his hands around the other boy's waist. They both begin to slide down the slide on their stomachs. Seeing the two boys sliding down feet first but facedown, a supervising teacher admonishes them to slide down "the right way" (feet first and faceup) and sends them to play in another area.

Admittedly, some risk of physical injury does exist anytime the play is very physical or rowdy. With appropriate safeguards, however, the risk of injury can be managed. The teacher in this vignette, concerned about the safety of the boys' play, might have responded differently. She could have moved closer to the play to better supervise it, and perhaps asked the boys, "What are you trying to do?" Once the teacher knew the boys' plan was to slide down staying connected, that they were not wrestling, she would have been better prepared to support their play while ensuring the children's safety. (Chapter 3 discusses managing versus eliminating risk in depth.)

The myth that rough-and-tumble play is aggression

Behind the fear of fighting and the fear of escalation is the belief that rough-and-tumble play is inherently an act of aggression. Many adults believe that such play supports the development of negative, aggressive behaviors, and this runs counter to their desire to instill peaceable values in young children.

Teachers, however, often misinterpret children's rough-and-tumble play as aggression (DiPietro 1981). Paquette and colleagues (2003) found

that teachers believe that one-third of play-fighting leads to real fighting when, in fact, play-fighting leads to real fighting in about one percent of play episodes.

One teacher noted,

> My co-teacher thinks that letting the kids play this roughly encourages aggression and more aggressive behavior. I do not agree. When the kids in my class roughhouse, they seem happy—they want to keep doing it. I'm always surprised that they do not hurt each other as much as I think they could.

Humphreys and Smith (1987) concluded that if such play was aggressive in nature, it would occur more often between play partners who dislike or who lack a preference for each other. They have found, however, that most rough-and-tumble play partners like each other, dismissing the belief that this type of play is inherently aggressive. Fry (1990) found that only one percent of aggressiveness in play resulted in injury to a participant, concluding that rough-and-tumble play is not generally aggressive in nature nor do the participants intend to harm each other.

Aggressive versus aggression

As children use powerful body movements to try to dominate each other, they also learn that complete domination runs counter to building successful relationships. Through the compromise involved in rough-and-tumble play, children learn more peaceable ways of relating.

A full understanding that rough-and-tumble play may sometimes be aggressive but is not an act of aggression starts with defining terms. *Aggressive* typically refers to actions that are assertive and pushy, that convey a desire to dominate or to win. Aggressive acts may be thought of as those that help someone be successful, like running faster to get to a tricycle. *Aggression*, on the other hand, is behavior that is "potentially harmful, intentionally inflicted, and aversive to the victim" (McEvoy et al. 2003, 53). An example of aggression is a child knocking another child out of the way in order to get to a tricycle.

Most young children engage in true physical aggression at some point in their early childhood. For example, a toddler who wants a doll from another child may try to pull it away first, and then may slap or bite the child in order to get the doll. A young preschooler who reaches a tricycle after another child may try to throw the first child off in order to have a turn. For typically developing children, physical aggression peaks between the ages of 2 and 4 and then declines (Benenson et al. 2008). Among children of the same age, teachers typically report more physical aggression from boys than from girls (Logue & Harvey 2010; McEvoy et al. 2003). But by age 4 or so, most children have learned the cognitive and social-emotional skills of language, turn taking, collaborating, boundary setting, and so on, that they need to interact successfully with others.

For a child to continue to be physically aggressive toward peers and others at age 4 and beyond is cause for concern and intervention. Physical aggression that persists is associated with a greater likelihood of future social difficulties, including juvenile delinquency and imprisonment (Farrington 2005). This inappropriate behavior could be the result of language delays, insecure attachment to a primary caregiver, or poorly developed social skills, for example. The key point here is: Because big body play supports social skill development, this aggressive play style can actually *help reduce* physical aggression in the long term.

Part of the confusion between what is rowdy play and what is real fighting arises because children's actions toward each other during play frequently mimic aggressive acts (Boulton 1993; DiPietro 1981). As children engage in rough-and-tumble play, they sometimes use *pretend aggression*. Pretend aggression is defined as "children exhibiting aggression in the context of make-believe, that includes children or doll characters acting out roles, children pretending to transform objects into other objects, or children creating objects and imaginary people" (Malloy & McMurray-Schwarz 2004, 237). Examples of pretend aggression are a child using table toys as a pretend gun or children playing cops and robbers.

Benenson and colleagues (2008) found that boys seem to derive pleasure from play that mimics actual physical aggression. In her research, Be-

---

Cultural Variations in Play

Young children in every culture engage in rough-and-tumble play, and such play often mimics the aggression children observe in their particular culture. For example, in the United States, where physical aggression is more prevalent in society overall than in some cultures, children's rough-and-tumble play is more physical.

However, in a culture such as the Semai, an indigenous people of central Malaysia who are nonaggressive, children have few models of physical aggression. As a result, the children's rough-and-tumble play is very mild compared with play in the United States. In Semai children's play, they may put their hands on each other's shoulders, but they rarely knock each other down. They tap toward each other with long sticks, but they rarely actually make physical contact (Fry 2005).

In sociodramatic big body play, the props children use may also reflect familiar culture experiences. Children in the United States, for example, may crawl on the ground and then bash into each other, mimicking race cars. Children in India may play a game called Chicken, in which they stand in lines directed at each other. In each line the children (the chickens) hold hands, while another child (the kite) takes turns swooping in on the children in line. The lines of chickens try to remain intact as the kite swoops in on each of them. When only one chicken is left, the kite and the chicken wrestle on the ground.

Regardless of the variance in cultural context and the socially derived props used in big body play, the signs that the children's play is just that—play, and not real fighting—are the same: laughter, smiles, or a relaxed face (Fry 2005).

nenson defined these play activities as "liking to play killing (soldier) and catching (police officer) people who have committed crimes" (157). Fifty-three percent of young respondents reported enjoying play that involved simulating these acts of aggression. Yet mimicking aggression does not typically lead to actual aggression (Malloy & McMurray-Schwarz 2004).

Distinguishing rough-and-tumble play from fighting

Although chasing, wrestling, and pushing may look like acts of aggression, especially to the untutored eye, 30 years of research have shown us that rough-and-tumble play is distinctly different from real fighting. The difference lies in children's intentions and in the context of their play.

In rough-and-tumble play, children's interactions are not intended to harm their playmates. Instead, their mutual goal is to extend the play for as long as possible. Children use their physical interactions to engage other

Policy and Rough-and-Tumble Play

Rough-and-tumble play—so often viewed as chaotic by teachers and parents—has been neglected and sometimes discouraged in standards and assessments.

In an early edition of NAEYC's own guide *Developmentally Appropriate Practice* (Bredekamp 1987), teachers were cautioned to recognize "signs of overstimulation such as when children . . . are carried away in chasing in wrestling," in order to prevent (rather than punish) the behavior (74). The *CDA Assessment Observation Instrument*, under "Guidance: Methods for Avoiding Problems," describes expectations for good practice: "Rough play is minimized. Example: defuses rough play before it becomes a problem; makes superhero play more manageable by limiting time and place" (Council for Professional Recognition 2007, 31).

Well-meaning in their efforts to protect children, such attempts to ban or limit children's rowdy play are based on the assumption that it typically escalates, or that children are typically injured while playing this way. As we have seen, neither assumption is true (Smith et al. 2004).

The most recent editions of *Developmentally Appropriate Practice in Early Childhood Programs* (Bredekamp & Copple 1997; Copple & Bredekamp 2009) reflect a greater understanding of and support for rough-and-tumble play. Such play is encouraged both indoors and outdoors, from infancy through 8 years of age. Teachers are encouraged to support children as they take risks in their play, to supervise them well to ensure safety, and to use children's play as the primary vehicle for cognitive, social, emotional, and physical development.

children and to work together on a play theme, which may be about dominance or control but uses turn taking and sharing as its tools. For example, when school-age children on the playground divide into teams to play Cops and Robbers, the dominant "cop" group tries to control the "robber" group. For the play to continue unabated, the groups must trade off so that each has a turn to be the dominant group. The context of the children's interaction is collaboration.

By contrast, in real fighting children use aggressive acts to coerce, to force their playmates to acquiesce to their desires. The context of the interaction is control. The physical aggression may involve striking another child with an object or a closed fist, instead of the open palm as often seen in play. In real fighting, even if the child uses an open palm, the strike is a hard slap.

Similarities observed between rough-and-tumble play and real aggression reflect completely different intentions (Hellendoorn & Harinck 1997). For example, children engaged in both acts may shove with an open palm (although children who are using their hands to inflict intentional harm usually use a fist). In play, however, a shove is given lightly and is not intended to control or inflict physical pain, and the children will take turns

For a child to continue to be physically aggressive toward peers and others at age 4 and beyond is cause for concern and intervention. Physical aggression that persists is associated with a greater likelihood of future social difficulties.

shoving each other. If the shove is an act of aggression, it will hurt, and the shoved child will usually cry and run away.

To enable children to play roughly without injury, teachers need to distinguish between appropriate, rough-and-tumble play and inappropriate, real fighting. The two have a different set of characteristics (Humphreys & Smith 1984), with three main distinctions:

1. Facial expressions. In appropriate, rough-and-tumble play, all of the children are smiling or at least exhibiting relaxed facial features. In real fighting, one child often initiates the attack and is generally grimacing or scowling. This child may stare at the other child before inflicting a blow. The aggressor child's facial movements are rigid, controlled, and stressed, and the jaw is usually clenched (Fry 2005). The other child often cries.

2. Willingness to participate. During rough-and-tumble play, all children are willing participants, and their intention is to have fun. In real fighting, however, the aggressor uses force to harm the other child, usually physically controlling that child in order to do so. The intention is to inflict pain or harm. Real fighting is often the result of a verbal challenge, such as "Make me!" or "I hate you!" Rough-and-tumble play, however, is the result of an invitation.

3. Willingness to return and extend the play. Children engaged in rough-and-tumble play return time and time again to it, with the goal of continuing and extending it (Boulton 1993; Fry 2005; Tannock 2008). They describe their play partners as their friends (Humphreys & Smith 1987). In real fighting, children on the receiving end of an attack typically flee the situation as soon as possible and do not voluntarily return for more (Carlson 2009). They may refuse to play with the aggressor for a period of time, and they name the child as someone they do not want to play with.

✳   ✳   ✳

It is not uncommon for adults, in well-intentioned efforts to supervise the young children in their care, to feel stress as they watch children engage in rough-and-tumble play. We focus on the hazards and pressures of keeping children safe. We feel anxious and unsure. But if we watch the faces of the children before us, we see joy.

> A group of boys about 6 years old were playing a rolling game on the grassy hill at my school. It progressed to gleefully falling on one another at an increasing frequency! The children had joyful, beaming faces. They were relaxed and happily chatting with one another on the way for water after the play had ended.

Children love this rough, rowdy play, and they need it. The next chapter discusses why.

Chapter 2

Benefits of Play, and Big Body Play in Particular

Play seems to have been especially adapted for the period of childhood, and is what children are "intended" to do. Remembering this may cause us to think twice before modifying children's environments to achieve one goal (e.g., more focused learning opportunities at schools) at the expense of play.

—Bjorklund and Pellegrini (2001, 331)

Children of all ages are in love with movement, action, and the self-empowerment that come from learning about, using, and gaining control over their bodies. The inherent draw to big body play only continues throughout the childhood years. It often is out of fear for children's safety that teachers and other adults try to stop children from the most physical forms of this play. Certainly, it's not from a blanket disregard for the benefits that physical activity provides. One study found that 90 percent of teachers and 86 percent of parents say that physically active children are better behaved and better able to learn in the classroom, and they are neither more active nor distracted in class *because of* having been physically active (Burdette & Whitaker 2005).

In other words, we adults know that physical activity in general is good for children. But maybe we just haven't taken stock of *how* good big body play in particular is. We may know the benefits of the gentle, quiet, cooperative forms of physical activity, such as rolling a ball back and forth or taking a nature walk or climbing the ladder to the slide. But what about the loud, rough, and rowdy forms? And are big body play's benefits primarily physical, or is development and learning of other types taking place, too?

As this chapter explains, play results in wonderful benefits across physical, social-emotional, and cognitive domains. It enhances problem-solving skills, creativity, and the ability to take another's perspective; reduces misbehavior; enhances language skills; and improves cognitive performance and social-emotional capacities (e.g., Barros et al. 2009; Singer et al. 2006). This chapter describes some of the benefits—both those unique to big body play (especially its rough-and-tumble forms) and those overlapping with the more generally acceptable forms of play such as sociodramatic.

What kind and how much physical activity?

There are two avenues to physical activity for young children: (1) the structured, directed kind that children get in a school physical education program and (2) the unstructured free play of big body play—the rough-and-tumble activities and the exuberant and spontaneous gross motor movements that come naturally and instinctively to children. Whereas big body play is recreational and child-led, physical education programs are adult-led and include meaningful content, instruction time, and assessment components (NASPE n.d.). Both types are important and valuable for children's health, kinesthetic intelligence, and overall development.

Both physical education programs and big body play can lead to vigorous exertion. Yet physical education programs, at least good ones, differ from play in at least two important ways: programs have goals and programs are planned, not spontaneous. The National Association for Sport and Physical Education (NASPE) provides guidance for providing both structured and unstructured physical activity, calibrated in developmentally appropriate amounts. (See chart.)

Although both structured and unstructured physical activity are valuable for young children, big body play typically produces greater *sustained* physical exertion, and so provides greater benefits. Children's big body play also tends to offer more *intensity* than does a movement period for toddlers or a physical education class in school. For example, one study of school-age children found that they got only 19 minutes of merely moderate activity in a 55-minute physical education class (Coe et al. 2006). (NASPE [2009b] recommends that for grades K to 2, a physical education class last just 30 minutes; for grade 3, the maximum is 45 minutes.)

Just 19 minutes is understandable considering that physical education programs require instruction time to explain rules, perhaps group manage-

NASPE Guidelines for Physical Activity

Guidelines for Infants

1. Infants should interact with caregivers in daily physical activities that are dedicated to explorin movement and the environment.
2. Caregivers should place infants in settings that encourage and stimulate movement experiences and active play for short periods of time several times a day.
3. Infants' physical activity should promote skill development in movement.
4. Infants should be placed in an environment that meets or exceeds recommended safety standards for performing large-muscle activities.
5. Those in charge of infants' well-being are responsible for understanding the importance of physical activity and should promote movement skills by providing opportunities for structured and unstructured physical activity.

Guidelines for Toddlers

1. Toddlers should engage in a total of at least 30 minutes of structured physical activity each day.
2. Toddlers should engage in at least 60 minutes—and up to several hours—per day of unstructured physical activity and should not be sedentary for more than 60 minutes at a time, except when sleeping.
3. Toddlers should be given ample opportunities to develop movement skills that will serve as the building blocks for future motor skillfulness and physical activity.
4. Toddlers should have access to indoor and outdoor areas that meet or exceed recommended safety standards for performing large-muscle activities.
5. Those in charge of toddlers' well-being are responsible for understanding the importance of physical activity and promoting movement skills by providing opportunities for structured and unstructured physical activity and movement experiences.

Guidelines for Preschoolers

1. Preschoolers should accumulate at least 60 minutes of structured physical activity each day.
2. Preschoolers should engage in at least 60 minutes—and up to several hours—of unstructured physical activity each day, and should not be sedentary for more than 60 minutes at a time, except when sleeping.
3. Preschoolers should be encouraged to develop competence in fundamental motor skills that will serve as the building blocks for future motor skillfulness and physical activity.
4. Preschoolers should have access to indoor and outdoor areas that meet or exceed recommended safety standards for performing large-muscle activities.
5. Caregivers and parents in charge of preschoolers' health and well-being are responsible for understanding the importance of physical activity and for promoting movement skills by providing opportunities for structured and unstructured physical activity.

Guidelines for Children Ages 5–8 (and older)

1. Children should accumulate at least 60 minutes, and up to several hours, of age-appropriate physical activity on all, or most days of the week. This daily accumulation should include moderate and vigorous physical activity with the majority of the time being spent in activity that is intermittent in nature.
2. Children should participate in several bouts of physical activity lasting 15 minutes or more each day.
3. Children should participate each day in a variety of age-appropriate physical activities designed to achieve optimal health, wellness fitness, and performance benefits.
4. Extended periods (periods of 2 hours or more) of inactivity are discouraged for children, especially during the daytime hours.

ment time, time waiting for others to play or perform, and maybe assessment time. Big body play, by contrast, typically proceeds uninterrupted. In fact, children may even protect the pace and flow of their play by refusing to allow time wasting by their playmates (e.g., too much talking) to interrupt the physical game (Jarvis 2007a).

Perhaps children know instinctively that they need uninterrupted time for intense activity to accrue the benefits associated with physical exertion. As NASPE (n.d.) notes, "Similar health benefits to those received during a physical education class are possible during physical activity bouts when the participant is active at an intensity that increases heart rate and produces heavier than normal breathing." What matters is the intensity and duration of the physical exertion; the result includes greater physical fitness and improved cognitive performance, among other benefits (Stevens et al. 2008).

There is a known connection between the development of movement and the development of cognition.

Evolution and brain development

From the United States to Kenya to the Philippines to Mexico, from ancient times to the Dark Ages to the present, in rats, orangutans, and humans, there is both anecdotal and empirical evidence of rough, rowdy physical play (e.g., Fry 1987, 2005; Groos 1901; Pellis et al. 1999).

Many theorize about why children universally engage in this type of play. Some feel the tumbling and rolling around is simply to let off steam. From an evolutionary developmental perspective, there is a notion that

play-fighting allows for the practice of adult roles; in part, in gender-specific ways. That is, big body play may help prepare children for the complex social aspects of what has been, evolutionarily speaking, adult life (Bjorklund & Pellegrini 2001). Others speculate that it is practice for future self-defense, that it supports the development of critical pathways in the brain vital for adaptive responses to aggression and dominance (Pellis & Pellis 2007).

Speculation aside, there is a known connection between the development of movement and the development of cognition (Diamond 2000), and researchers believe there is a connection between the very physical, rowdy play style and critical periods of brain development (Byers 1998). The rough play between peers appears to be critical for individuals to learn how to calibrate their movements and orient themselves physically in appropriate and adaptive ways (Pellis et al. 1999).

There also is evidence that rough-and-tumble play leads to the release of chemicals affecting the mid-brain, lower forebrain, and the cortex, including areas responsible for decision making and social discrimination; growth chemicals positively affect development of these brain areas. Furthermore, there is evidence that severe deprivation of such play (or damage to related areas of the brain) is associated with a failure to adjust behavior to idiosyncrasies of a partner's social status and movements (Pellis & Pellis 2007). In other words, rough-and-tumble play, this universal activity of all children throughout history and in all parts of the world, is adaptive, evolutionarily useful, and linked to normal brain development.

Growing and moving

Through big body play, children learn skills such as how their bodies move in space, where parts of their bodies begin and end, and how to control their physical movements. It is also an effective way for young children to have their physical touch needs met, when the play is both individually appropriate (i.e., comfortable for a given child) and age-appropriate (Carlson 2006; Reed 2005).

Skeletal and muscular development in infancy

Infants gain obvious gross motor benefits from the rough play they enjoy using their own bodies and the bodies of their peers and caregivers. A human infant is born possessing all the muscle fibers he or she will ever have. These fibers are small, however, with a high ratio of water and fat to muscle. As the child grows and develops, the ratio changes and muscle strength increases (Boyd & Bee 2006). Also, a newborn's leg bones are too soft to support his or her body weight. This lack of muscle strength combined with too-soft leg bones means that infants are floor-bound for the majority of their first year.

Because infants can engage in big body play even while they lack muscle and bone strength, such unstructured, very active play is ideal in supporting their emerging physical capabilities. Long stretches of spontaneous reaching, grabbing, kicking, waving, rolling, and scooting all develop an infant's bone and muscle strength. There is evidence, moreover, that whereas low-birthweight premature infants usually lose bone strength after birth, even brief range-of-motion activity can prevent the problem, allowing for more normal bone development—even in the first few weeks of life (Litmanovitz et al. 2003).

Participation in regular physical activity also helps prevent chronic health problems, such as diabetes, high blood pressure, and high cholesterol, even in very young children.

Physical health

Young children rarely remain vigorously active for an hour straight, as an exercising adult or older child engaged in an organized sport might do. Young children's spontaneous physical play tends to come in very active bursts lasting from 5 to 15 minutes. Nonetheless, those bursts add up and accumulate into health benefits that are similar to those for older children and adults.

When young children have the opportunity to play in rough, active, highly physical ways, they get their heart rates up; they stretch their limbs; they strengthen their bones, muscles, and ligaments; they burn calories and maintain a healthy weight; and they learn new physical skills, all of which contribute hugely to their fundamental health and optimal growth.

As Pellegrini and Smith (1998a) noted, "Play may be the only way [young children] are likely to get sufficient exercise training, at least before organized games and sports, in human societies" (610).

Studies are clear about the benefits of physical activity in promoting physical health and general well-being (e.g., Sola et al. 2010). Children who are active—running, jumping, throwing, climbing—do better on tests of physical fitness, in areas including endurance, speed, agility, balance, and strength. They also show a reduced body mass index, which measures overall body fat, and better oxygen intake. They are less likely to be overweight or obese, which is a common and pressing American problem at present, in part as a result of children's sedentary lifestyles. Participation in regular physical activity also helps prevent chronic health problems, such as diabetes, high blood pressure, and high cholesterol, even in very young children (Ward 2010).

Preschool and beyond: Discovering size, strength, and control

Through big body play, children in the preschool years and beyond become more aware of their own physical abilities: *how strong they are, how fast they are, how heavy they are.* Part of children's success at rough-and-tumble play results from their ability to control their body movements so that neither they nor their play partners are hurt (Paquette et al. 2003). For example, the motions of rough-and tumble play are mostly tagging and wrestling moves that either completely avoid body contact ("You missed me!") or that make contact in a way that does not cause injury or harm. And even though it is generally friends who play together this way, they are often of unequal body weight, size, and strength.

Leaping expresses faith in yourself and in your environment. The opportunity to jump from different heights and land safely is incomparable, a test of self and gravity (Greenman 2007, 292).

So, how do children develop the skills of knowing their own strength and then, if necessary, restraining themselves for the sake of the play and their relationships? They learn by participating in the give-and-take of rough-and-tumble play, which provides immediate feedback. Take this scenario:

> Two preschool boys are throwing a ball back and forth on the playground. One calls to the other, "Want to wrestle?" The other boy says, "Sure!" So, the boys fall to the ground, put their arms around each other, and begin to wrestle. The larger boy rolls on top and pins the smaller boy to the ground. The smaller boy pushes against the larger boy's chest, and the larger boy jumps up, saying, "I'll let you go first next time, cause I'm bigger."

The larger boy was immediately aware of his physical advantage. He also realized that if he wanted the enjoyable wrestling play to continue, he needed to make some provision for his larger size and greater strength. So he decided to hold back some (called *self-handicapping*) and allow the smaller boy to strike first, so the match could proceed more fairly and so last longer. The experience provided both children feedback on their relative size and strength.

Feeling and interacting

Big body play also enhances social development as children learn turn taking, self-handicapping, and collaborative play in games with rules. They learn social skills through accepting dominant and subordinate roles, negotiating, and developing and maintaining friendships. Big body play promotes cooperation and compromise (Boulton & Smith 1992).

Social-emotional development in infancy and toddlerhood

Through the active, unstructured, very physical interactions babies and toddlers have with their own bodies, other babies, and adults, they learn an incredible amount about themselves, their bodies, and the world (McCune 1998). Based on this knowledge of self and the world, the interac-

tions build a foundation for critical emotional abilities. In big body play, an important emphasis is on what the infant is learning about his or her own body (Sheets-Johnstone 2008).

Self-concept, meaning a person's knowledge about himself or herself, generally starts developing at about 1 to 2 years old (Houck & Spegman 1999). In the sensorimotor phase, children at this age move independently and act on their own. They will start to recognize themselves in a mirror or picture, and soon can verbally articulate awareness of themselves as entities independent from their mother and others around them. Then they begin demonstrating self-conscious emotions, such as embarrassment and pride (Houck 1999).

But this self-concept all begins with an awareness of their physical body. Differentiated cries and certain physical reactions, such as kicking in protest, indicate that a baby is developing a self-concept. The ability to represent and reflect on one's own body explicitly and objectively may be a unique dimension of early development, a distinct component of objective self-awareness that emerges in toddlerhood (Brownell et al. 2007).

Once very young children are aware of how movement affects their own bodies, they are then able to develop a sense of how their movements can affect others. *Empathy* is the combined ability of being able to interpret what another person is feeling and then to experience related emotions yourself (Light et al. 2009). It begins with an understanding of oneself and one's own reactions and responses. As infants gain awareness of their own feelings, they are able to interpret others' feelings and match them. In empathy, according to Sheets-Johnstone (2008), "We basically make sense of each other in ways outside language. In this sense making, movement is our match-point" (194). In this physical way, then, empathy is born.

Consider the following scenario:

> Six-month-olds Zoe and Nate are on a blanket on the floor, Zoe on her back and Nate on his stomach. Zoe flips over and lands on Nate's arm. After several seconds of having Zoe's weight on his arm, Nate begins to cry, vigorously kicking his feet and legs as he does. Alarmed by Nate's cries and kicks, Zoe stares at him for several seconds, then rolls over. Now Nate is completely underneath her.
> Zoe wiggles, scoots, and smiles. Nate continues to cry and kick. She rolls off him. Nate quiets and rolls over onto another area of the blanket.

In this scenario, both babies experience many physical sensations, including the feel and weight of each other's bodies against their own. Nate is unhappy with the sensation of Zoe's body weight first on his arm and then on his chest. Judging by his cries and kicks, he finds its heaviness extremely uncomfortable. When Zoe rolls off, Nate feels the pressure relieved.

For her part, Zoe experiences the feeling of Nate's arm and body underneath her, the sounds of his cries, and the pressure of his feet and legs kicking against her. When she rolls away, Zoe feels flat, firm ground underneath her. Both experience the cessation of Nate's cries.

Through these multiple sensations and the act of initiating various behaviors (e.g., crying, kicking, rolling away), the babies added to their awareness of self and another; the experience was informative and useful, even though not entirely pleasant. They learned about their own sensations and added to their emerging self-concepts, experiencing the beginnings of empathy.

Preschool and beyond: Self-restraint and reciprocity

As children enter the kindergarten and primary years, they want to practice emerging social skills such as fairness and reciprocity (turn taking); big body play provides rich opportunities for practicing those. Children become aware of the consequences of failing to harness or handicap their own strengths if the opponent is smaller or weaker. So although rough-and-tumble play looks to be an activity of physical dominance, it actually prompts children to learn how to hold back physically, how to restrain themselves for the sake of the play and their relationships. Successful rough-and-tumble play depends on reciprocity.

Although rough-and-tumble play looks to be an activity of physical dominance, it actually prompts children to learn how to restrain themselves for the sake of the play and their relationships.

Children who play this way with each other usually are already friends, and the rough-and-tumble play can enhance their relationship by supporting the skills needed in strong friendships. Just as no one wants a friend who takes all the time or attention, or who dominates the whole conversation, no child wants a rough-and-tumble play partner who dominates the whole activity.

Most successful play experiences, like successful relationships, are successful because both partners know how to wait, how to give and take, and how to listen as well as talk. In big body play, children have opportunities to practice and begin to master these skills. For example, consider a group of children playing King of the Hill. In order for the play to continue, the children have to take turns being the "King" as well as being the ones rolled down the hill. If the King never exchanged roles with the other children, most of them would tire quickly of always being the ones rolled and would quit the game.

Or, consider a wrestling bout. If one child were always to end up on the bottom, that child would soon no longer want to wrestle. Both children quickly learn that to keep things fun and interesting and to ensure they have someone to wrestle with, they must take turns being on the bottom. They also learn that in offering to be on the bottom, someone else gets to be on the top. And in offering to go last, someone else gets to go first. Waiting to be on top or go first is rewarded by the friendship and the continued play.

Preschool and beyond: Assertiveness

Children also learn another important social skill through rough-and-tumble play: how to stand up for themselves when necessary (Paquette et al. 2003). Although children will realize that backing down and compromising are the most socially successful routes in most cases, there are times when assertiveness will be the right choice. Because rough-and-tumble play gives children opportunities to feel and know their own strength, they will feel more confident when a situation demands some dominance or limit setting from them.

For example, a child might need to assert when the play has gone on too long or when he has had enough:

> Andy and Evan are rolling around on the playground. For several minutes, they wrap their arms around each other and roll side-to-side the length of the playground. Andy begins to tire of the play and starts to get up. Evan wants to continue, so he reaches to pull him back. Andy, who wants to stop, firmly says, "No!" Evan releases him, and he stands and walks away.

Socially Rejected or Awkward Children

As beneficial as rough-and-tumble play is for children with typically developing social skills, it is of as much and perhaps even more value for children whose social skills lag. Big body play provides opportunities for "socially rejected" children—those who lack the social skills needed to form successful relationships—to experience and practice the very skills they lack: turn taking, understanding nonverbal signals and body language, using words to communicate emotions and desires, boundary setting, and a strong sense of self.

Unfortunately for these children, though, without these same skills as precursors, rough-and-tumble play is difficult, sometimes impossible, for them. Socially rejected children often misunderstand the playful intent of their playmates' tags and jabs and respond to them in a hostile manner. Indeed, rough-and-tumble play is 25 times more likely to become real fighting when socially rejected children are among the participants (Schafer & Smith 1996; Smith et al. 2004).

Because of this more frequent escalation of friendly play into aggression and sometimes violent play, teachers are hesitant to allow socially rejected children to engage in rough-and-tumble play, fearing—and perhaps rightly so—that someone will get hurt.

What research shows, however, is that "it may not be the case that the more socially competent children engage in more play-fighting, but rather that the play-fighting may promote the development of social competency" (Pellis & Pellis 2007, 97). In other words, it's possible that socially savvy children don't come to the play already that way; they get that way *from* the play.

In this scenario, the interaction provided the tired boy a chance to practice successful boundary setting, engendering confidence in his own decision making and self-efficacy.

Communicating

Big body play enhances language development as children use and learn to understand nonverbal communication. It also helps them to understand the reciprocal nature of language in conversation, practiced so beautifully in the reciprocal nature of rough-and-tumble play. Children learn language skills through signals and nonverbal communication, including the ability to perceive, infer, and decode.

Differentiated cries and gestures in infancy

The motions and gestures that infants often use to communicate with adults and with other infants demonstrate the emergence of pre-linguistic skills. Such signaling is the way children begin to express their needs, beginning in infancy (Paquette et al. 2003).

One of the main contributions of big body play to children's development is the way it supports nonverbal communication through its use of signals.

For example, the sound of a cry that a baby makes when in the physical discomfort of being rolled on by another baby is different from the cry expressing fatigue or hunger. Babies experiencing the displeasure of a physical sensation might also kick their legs, as Nate did in the earlier vignette, or push or wave their arms. And babies experiencing joy in the interaction might coo or smile or close their eyes. By smiling and wiggling, for example, Zoe signaled that she enjoyed the sensation of being off the ground and on Nate's body.

The differentiated cries, coos, facial expressions, and actions such as kicking provide the infant the opportunity to practice communicating. This use of both verbal and nonverbal communication provides the foundation for later language learning.

Preschool and beyond: Signals and nonverbal communication

One of the main contributions of big body play to children's development is the way it supports nonverbal communication through its use of signals (Bjorklund & Brown 1998; Paquette et al. 2003). When one child wants to invite another child to join the play, for example, she may signal by waving or gesturing "come here." During the course of the play, children might signal for the play partner to stop (holding out both hands in front, palms and fingers up), or for the partner to get up or get off (both hands placed firmly against the other child), or for the other to move or go the other direction (hands waving back and forth, or fingers swirling in a circular motion).

The most often used signal in rough-and-tumble play, and the one that seems to universally signify the playful nature of these very physical interactions, is the "play face." Children smile when they are playing in a friendly and appropriate way. Their smiles signal their acceptance and enjoyment of the play. It is what clearly denotes rough-and-tumble play *as* play rather than as aggression, sending an unmistakable signal that the child finds the experience welcoming and joyful.

Children also use their eyes to signal desire and intent. For example, a child who is enjoying the play might close her eyes while laughing. In contrast, a child experiencing pain or displeasure would widen her eyes or begin to stare.

When children learn to decode such signals, their ability to succeed socially is enhanced (Pellegrini & Smith 1998b). As friendships begin to form during the preschool years, successful communication is foundational to these budding friendships. When children know how to correctly "read" and understand what others are communicating through their eyes or gestures or facial expressions, each child is better able to form strong friendships.

Preschool and beyond: Negotiation, narration, and other language skills

In addition to strengthening decoding and nonverbal skills, rough-and-tumble play provides a unique opportunity for strengthening verbal skills, particularly negotiating and narrating. Because young children are not natural turn takers, they often have to discuss "the rules" or the plans for the play before they begin, and they discuss how to adjust things as they go. To succeed at this, they must use and master early negotiation skills as they play with their peers.

In the following vignette, for example, one boy verbalizes a plan for play that allows the game to proceed without fighting or distress:

> After a group of children decide to hang upside down from a climbing structure, they have to decide who will go first, next, and so on. Several children, of course, want to go first. Dante offers that, "Once we start going, then everybody will get to be first," meaning that the next child in line will always then be "first" after the child at the front of the line goes. Some of the children are understandably skeptical. Once the line begins to move, though, they see that he is correct—each child now has a turn being "first" in line.

The practice of developing narratives to go along with the play is an important bridge to later involvement in sports and other socially competitive activities that are language based.

This example demonstrates very basic negotiation, wherein all the children witnessed one boy's ability to find and offer a solution and to communicate it effectively to the others. The situation provided a chance for Dante to practice his communication skills. And it set an example for the less socially skilled children to learn from and follow.

As games become more complex amongst older young children, the rules they negotiate, and how they do so, become more complex, as well. Jarvis (2007a) even refers to a "rule-negotiation culture" in emphasizing how absorbed young children become in creating and adhering to the rules of their self-made games (256).

The tendering of rules is often embedded in a narrative, which can be a fantasy, an explanation of the activity, or a way to augment the events taking place—all ways to connect thoughts and actions through language. Developmentally, the practice of developing narratives to go along with the play is an important bridge to later involvement in sports and other socially competitive activities that are language based. After the preschool ages, there is a metamorphosis from the more impulsive, chaotic rowdy play into more formalized games with simple (and even later, elaborate) child-developed rules (Jarvis 2007a; Pellegrini 1989).

Interestingly, there typically are quite specific gender differences in the narrations, indicating that big body play either contributes to or reveals, or both, the diverging development of boys and girls. Jarvis (2007a), in a study of 4- and 5-year-olds, found that boys and girls created different types of stories with highly specific gender roles. Girls' narratives around their play tended to show competition for being the nicest, whereas boys' narratives emphasized their toughness. The narratives might involve role-playing of animals, fairy tale characters, popular media characters, and so forth, providing plenty of practice for improving on children's growing language skills.

Thinking

From infancy onward, big body play enhances cognitive development, improving young children's problem-solving and spatial skills, attention, and achievement.

Locomotion and exploration in infancy

Movement and the tactile exploration that come with big body play both foster learning in infants. Basic locomotion activities—cruising, crawling, sitting, pulling to stand, and other big body movements—teach an infant about her own body in relation to her environment. With opportunities for physical experiences, she can know where she is in relation to objects and other things simply by looking around and making a connection between her visual and physical experiences (Uchiyama et al. 2008).

When infants bang objects with their hands, throw or mouth objects, squeeze a ball, or reach for and grab fabrics, toys, and each other, they are exhibiting curiosity, a hallmark of healthy cognitive development. When we support their body movements, we support their curiosity and learning (Honig 2009).

Preschool and beyond: Problem-solving skills

At times, big body play requires complex decision-making and problem-solving skills. Problem solving is required because children must first pay attention, then plan, organize, sequence, and make decisions about what they will play and how. One study of kindergarten-age boys showed that the amount of time spent in active social play with other boys directly predicted their problem-solving skills a year later (Pellegrini & Blatchford 2000).

How might this connection between active social play and skill development work? Say a group of preschoolers want to hang upside down from the top rung of a ladder on a piece of climbing equipment on their playground. Several problem-solving steps are involved to achieve the play:

They first see the rung (*pay attention*), then they begin to discuss how to hang from it (*plan*). The hanging from it part is difficult because it will require a child to be able to pull a leg up and over the rung, and then pull the other leg up and over the rung, all while still hanging on the rung. One child begins to do this. He is successful, and swings upside down for several seconds before grabbing the rung with his hands, swinging his legs around, and dropping to the ground. The next three children all have difficulty.

They discuss their difficulty, and decide to ask for help (*organizing*) from the teacher—who has been closely supervising this activity. Each child tells the teacher what kind of support he or she needs, saying things such as, "Help me hold on" or "Now help me pull my foot out" (*sequencing*). One child, after several attempts, decides the task is too hard, and he decides to climb down (*decision making*).

Throughout rough-and-tumble play, children have to make assessments about their own capacities; about their play partners' capacities

and relative size, speed, or strength; about their partners' ability to decode signals and capitulate; about how to get out of an uncomfortable situation; about how to achieve what peers or older children achieve; about what to say, and how to say it, to enhance the play; about helping a weaker or less competent peer; about when to engage an adult; and so forth.

Rough-and-tumble play provides unique opportunities to practice all kinds of problem-solving skills. Exercising these skills might seem to be simply about competition and dominance. In fact, the skills have been shown to allow children to explore the complex dynamics of justice mediation and peacekeeping (Holland 2003). The social components of rough-and-tumble play have positive implications for the development of the individual, the harmony of the group, and solidarity amongst peers and within children's community at large.

Preschool and beyond: Spatial skills

Researchers have speculated that gender differences in the types of physical play that children choose may shed light on the links between rough-and-tumble play and cognitive development, specifically spatial skills (Bjorklund & Brown 1998). Silverman and Eals (1992) suggested that a gender division in labor in ancient times   males being more involved in hunting and navigation and females more involved in foraging—may have led to an evolution of gender differences that shows up in spatial abilities *and* physical play.

For example, boys tend to choose activities that require hand-eye coordination, such as football or climbing on trees or equipment; and boys tend to perform better than girls on cognitive tasks that require mental rotation and involve spatial relations. Girls tend to perform better on tasks requiring fine motor skills and on object-location memory tasks (Silverman & Eals 1992). Likewise, in a study of preschoolers, researchers again found gender differences in spatial abilities, and a significant, positive correlation between the amount of time spent on spatial activities while playing and performance on tests of spatial abilities (Connor & Serbin 1977).

Some types of big body play require a great deal of spatial ability, such as estimating how fast to run to which spot to kick a soccer ball, or thinking through and enacting the complex plays one sees on a basketball court, or in the similar made-up games young children devise. These games involving big body play contribute to improved spatial skills, and the more children (of both sexes) use those skills, the better they get (Bjorklund & Brown 1998).

Use the elements of movement—space, shape, force, flow, time, and rhythm—to encourage children to discover various ways to perform skills. If children are jumping around the playground or classroom, ask them playfully to try jumping backward, sideways, or around in circles; while being very big or very small; with pauses in between; and slowly or quickly (Pica 2006, 78).

Rough-and-Tumble Play for Boys

In aggressive sports, the opposing player congratulates hard, clean hits. This knowledge begins at an early age where fathers are rolling around on the floor with their infant sons.

—Reed and Brown 2000, 335

Rough-and-tumble play is good for all children, but it seems to have a strong and special draw for boys in particular. They engage in it more often than girls, they develop boys-only games and cultures around it, and there may be unique benefits of rough-and-tumble play for them.

That boys engage more than girls do in contact-oriented rough-and-tumble play is well-established (Carson et al. 1993; DiPietro 1981; Humphreys & Smith 1984). There is certainly plenty of mixed-gender rough play, but boys tend to initiate rough-and-tumble play more often and girls tend to withdraw from it sooner (Fabes 1994; Meany et al. 1985; Pellis et al. 1996). Also, starting by age 4 or so, boys tend to self-group in boys-only games, whereas girls tend to segregate themselves from the boys' games (Fabes 1994; Jarvis 2007a). Also, when boys are deprived of opportunities for active physical play, they are especially active when they do get to play compared with girls, who are less so (Pellegrini & Smith 1998a).

Why should such a difference exist? It may be biological, at least in part, since levels of testosterone have a clear influence on how much children of both sexes engage in very physical play, and of course, boys have higher levels of testosterone than girls (Hines et al. 2002). It may also in part be cultural, as boys practice defending their turf and protecting their territory; some would even argue these games are a precursor to a sense of nationalism and patriotism in adulthood (O'Donnell & Sharpe 2004). Jarvis (2007a) studied a group of kindergarten-age boys playing soccer and wrote:

> Although I never observed any discussion between the children on this point, the division of territory between the age cohorts within the school (with the field split into rough quarters) was never disregarded during the times of my observations; the children appeared to have a firm, implicitly agreed sense of where "their" territory began and ended. (251)

As noted in the section on cognitive thinking, there is also a link between boys' choices of physical play activities and their performance on spatial-skills tests, perhaps lending support to an evolutionary perspective on rough-and-tumble play.

Yet perhaps the most moving and compelling aspects of rough-and-tumble play for boys are found in the social dynamics of the interactions that exist only within boys-only rough play. Boys learn from each other how to show care and concern, how to protect others, how to assert and defend themselves in socially successful ways, how to play out stories and fantasies in what Jordan (1995, 76) calls a "warrior discourse," how to negotiate rules, and how to touch each other in male-acceptable ways.

Consider this description of boys in kindergarten to early primary grades in the United Kingdom playing "football" (soccer in the United States):

> The boys clearly showed care and concern towards each other in order not to exclude regular members of the footballing group. When Rory was recovering from a broken arm and was not supposed to engage in rough football for the week after his cast was taken off, the other boys playing football encouraged him to join in, made a point of passing to him and refrained from tackling him when he had the ball. A subtle signalling system was also observed that allowed the football players to show approval towards one another, a light tap on the back, usually administered by a slightly older boy to a boy who had taken a heavy fall or a minor injury without making a fuss. (Jarvis 2007a, 252)

There are clear mentoring relationships among the boys, wherein the older or more socially adept boys subtly teach the younger or less mature boys how to display toughness while simultaneously showing awareness and care about others' well-being. Through rough-and-tumble play, boys learn that it is okay to jump up and down and hug when a goal is scored—but not when you get hurt. They also learn how not to touch their friends (e.g., no holding hands) and how and when to touch their friends (e.g., a light tap on the back after a score or after showing toughness). Through rough-and-tumble play, boys learn and practice ways of expressing a masculine type of intimacy that is reserved for male-to-male friendships.

Being tough is a critical ingredient for social success for boys. It relates to peer status, to popularity, and to leadership roles within peer groups (Hartup 1983; Pellegrini,1995; Strayer 1980; Vaugn & Waters 1981). Boys use rough-and-tumble play as a unique means both of discovering their toughness for themselves and of establishing their tough reputation amongst their peers. And all of this must be done in a way that preserves friendships. Boys have to learn how to show they are stronger and faster than other boys, while also showing they know how to hold back on their strength or speed so as not to hurt a friend. It is a complicated and sophisticated process, ever dynamic as relative physical strengths change and as social and emotional skills emerge and change.

—Heather Biggar Tomlinson

Preschool and beyond: Attention and achievement

Bjorklund and Brown (1998) put it plainly when they wrote, "Despite the social consequences of [rough-and-tumble] activity, the mechanisms involved are every bit as 'cognitive' as are those associated with math seat-work" (604). Vigorous physical activity, the kind that is associated with unstructured big body play, indeed has a relationship to cognitive and academic performance (Tomporowski et al. 2008).

Big body play gets children's blood going and minds moving, or rather, gets the mind settled; it has been linked to better attention and concentration skills in school (Hillman et al. 2005; Shephard 1996; Taras 2005). By providing regular opportunities for physical activity and at least an hour a day for sustained, moderate to vigorous, unstructured physical play, adults not only support healthy big body play but also support children's periods of quiet attention: Children tend to remain calm for longer periods of time following the very active play (Scott & Panksepp 2003).

A new kindergarten teacher shared his experience:

> I was teaching my heart out, but I did not feel that my students were learning. They were constantly touching each other, pulling hair, rolling on the floor, standing up, and playing with their jackets and clothes. Then one day, I told myself that I had tried things the conventional way, and now I was going to try things my way. From then on, I had my students up and moving. We sang songs and marched around the room to learn the days of the week and the months of the year. We did daily physical exercises. We did math by creating patterns with our bodies, such as *snap, clap, stomp* and *jump, run, wiggle*. We did skip-counting using hip hop music that the kids were familiar with. After a few days of this, my students were able to sit and listen during the times that required them to do so. They were not touching each other, pulling hair, rolling on the floor, standing up, or playing with their jackets and clothes. My kids were learning, and they were happy. True teaching was taking place.

Recent studies examining thousands of children show that active physical activity and play are related to better performance in both reading and mathematics (Grissom 2005; Stevens et al. 2008).

As previously noted, it seems to be that it is vigorous, active play—rather than a traditional physical education curriculum per se, which may not provide an intense bout of activity—that is associated with higher academic performance (Coe et al. 2006). Children's self-determined rough-and-tumble play is good for the mind as well as the body.

✳   ✳   ✳

Boisterous, rowdy, loud, vigorous, rough, exuberant, and always physical in nature, big body play is the naturally occurring play style that gives children the opportunities they need for overall optimum development.

While sitting increases fatigue and reduces concentration, movement feeds oxygen, water, and glucose to the brain, optimizing its performance (Pica 2006, 112).

From birth, children gather enormous information from their bodies. They learn about themselves, and about how they affect the environment and others in it. This self-knowledge and world knowledge forms the foundation for future exploration and learning. This foundation, built on ample opportunities to learn about their own bodies, boundaries, strength, needs, abilities, power, and control, can provide young children the physical, social-emotional, and thinking skills to have healthy, rewarding experiences and successful relationships in early childhood and throughout their lives.

Hanging from the monkey bars and playing Tag and soccer is a kind of serious business. But it's not the process that is serious—playing is resolutely *not* serious—it's the results that are serious, in a good way. As much as children need rough, rowdy play for staying physically fit, they need it even more to learn about the complex social dynamics amongst friends and peers, to gain problem-solving experience, to practice empathy and negotiation skills, and to be ready to sit and focus inside the classroom when that is required.

As discussed in the next chapter, if we adults can provide the time, space, and encouragement for safe big body play, we will be rewarded. We will see children who show delight and exuberance; who are spontaneous and creative in their play; who can "run wild" and then sit calmly, ready to focus; and who are confident in themselves and selfless toward their peers.

Chapter 3

Strategies for Implementing Big Body Play

I allow rough-and-tumble play in my classroom. Last year I had 15 active boys. To help them focus their play, I set out mats on the grass, gave them foam blocks, and let them go at it. Before we started, I role-played with a parent to show the kids how to watch for social cues and explained the rules for hitting (tagging—no closed fists or punches). When I saw one child look distressed, I stopped the play, and we talked about body language. With practice and continued guidance, they were able to engage in this play safely and frequently asked for it.

—Early childhood teacher

Even when teachers and program directors understand what big body play is (and is *not*) and its many physical, social-emotional, and cognitive benefits to children, some may still hesitate to support it in their classrooms and on the playground (Smith et al. 2004). They should be reassured that it is possible to implement big body play safely. How to do so is the topic of this chapter.

Managing risk

Banning big body play for fear that children might get hurt involves a misperception about risk taking in general. Certainly, teachers and parents should and do place the highest priority on children's safety and well-being. But part of the well-documented value of play to learning and development is directly related to the risks children face in their play and the physical and social problem solving they must do to navigate those risks successfully. Little (2006) wrote,

> If adults make decisions that deny children the opportunity to engage in risky activities, children are also being denied the opportunity to learn about risk and how to evaluate risks. The ability to identify and appropriately manage risks is an important life skill that children need to learn. (151)

So, what do we mean by *risk?* Although the term can carry a negative connotation, "the assessment of risk is actually on a continuum that can be both positive and negative. Risk is managed by finding a risk level that is appropriate and acceptable" (Mitchell et al. 2006, 122).

Positive risk

For example, a child climbing up a rope ladder incurs the risk of falling. If the ladder is 10 feet high and the ground below the ladder is bare and hard, a fall is very likely to be injurious. Allowing a child to climb that rope ladder involves disproportionately *negative* risk and is unacceptable; that is, the potential for harm outweighs any positive potential outcome. If, however, it is a 6-foot ladder and there is a deep layer of shock-absorbing ground cover below, the risk is now *positive*—one managed to prevent major physical harm, with the potential for the child to experience positive physical gains from climbing, as well as positive emotional gains from making the effort and succeeding.

High-quality early childhood programs offer children opportunities for challenging physical activities every day because the potential physical, social-emotional, and cognitive benefits of the activities outweigh the likelihood of being hurt. Little (2006) reinforced this point:

> Early childhood educators are charged with the responsibility of fostering development. . . . It is necessary, therefore, for teachers to find a balance between the positive and negative forms of risk taking that enable children to learn and practice necessary skills whilst minimizing the possibility of injury. (145–46)

Some early childhood communities have responded to the challenge of managing risk by attempting to *eliminate* it—by banishing any activity or equipment that poses the possibility of physical injury. Their focus has been on preventing *any* injury rather than on preventing serious injury while providing children with appropriate risk opportunities (Little 2006; Stephenson 2003). One early childhood teacher, posting to an educational listserv, shared his perspective on this overcompensation:

> I recently came back from an overnight field trip—but nothing really happened. Not one of the 24 kids did fall in the water, not one did cut or

Forty-six percent of preschool programs surveyed reported having a no-tolerance policy toward rough-and-tumble play (Logue & Harvey 2010).

> ### Regulations and Rough-and-Tumble Play
>
> State licensing regulations do not always support risk-taking behaviors or the increased supervision needed to accommodate activities such as rough-and-tumble play. In Georgia, for example, the November 2010 revision of the state's child care regulations (Georgia Department of Early Care and Learning 2011) included a rule change to state, "Staff shall not engage in, or allow children or other adults to engage in, activities that could be detrimental to a child's health or well-being, such as but not limited to horse play, rough play, wrestling. . . ." (591-1-1-.03 Activities). Although children's well-being certainly is the rationale for such regulations, these same regulations (591-1-1-.32 Staff:Child Ratios and Supervision) allow group sizes and staff-child ratios—factors also closely connected to children's well-being—that are higher than those recommended as a standard of good practice in NAEYC's Accreditation Criteria for Standard 10: Leadership and Management.
>
> To support big body play in group care and classroom settings, staff-child ratios should be low enough to provide for the constant supervision this play generally requires. Part of our role as early childhood educators is to advocate for young children. Study what your state regulations say about rough-and-tumble play and its place in high-quality early childhood settings, and work toward amending those regulations, if necessary, so that all children can have access to this invaluable play.

bruise, no one was crying. It does sound like the perfect trip! . . . So why am I not satisfied? Some years ago, there would have been bandages, comforting words. John would fall. Peter would slide. Lisa would have a pretty scary cut, and so on. But all three kids would have described the trip as "the best ever!"

With appropriate planning and supervision, rough-and-tumble play activities can remain safe as well as enjoyable. Concrete strategies are discussed in more detail later in this chapter.

Risk versus hazard

When discussing risk taking in general, and the value of risk taking in early childhood education in particular, it is important to distinguish risk from hazard. A *risk* involves the possibility of suffering harm or loss and can be managed through planning and supervision. A *hazard* involves danger or calamity and must be avoided—also through planning and supervision.

For example, letting toddler Daniel walk on his own around the house is risky—he might fall and bump his head. A parent might manage this risk by staying close to Daniel as he toddles around. Allowing 6-year-old Audrey to ride her bicycle in the driveway is also risky; she might run into Mom's car and hurt herself. Mom might manage this risk by parking the car on the street or in the garage while Audrey is riding her bike. But leaving Daniel to wander while the parent talks on the phone, or letting Audrey ride on a busy street, is hazardous; the risks involved cannot be managed.

This distinction between risk and hazard is crucial. Without it, it is easy to view as hazardous all activities that involve even a slight chance that a child could be hurt, and to ban those activities. Many classroom activities and materials, however, can pose a hazard to children if not properly supervised. For example, wooden blocks make excellent three-dimensional structures, but they also carry enough weight to inflict a serious injury if a child uses one to strike another child. Tricycles give children the opportunity to develop balance and pedaling skills, but children often fall off as they are riding and skin their knees. The risks posed by these activities are managed through planning and supervision. So it is with big body play. Such play is a *risk* to be managed, not a *hazard* to be eliminated.

To provide for rough-and-tumble play while managing the risk associated with it, teachers and directors can do three things: (1) set policies

that support the play in the curriculum, (2) prepare both the indoor and outdoor environments to ensure children's safety, and (3) provide support and supervision to enable children to take the risks they need for healthy development.

Establishing policies for safe, effective big body play

Establishing program policies for big body play is vital to ensure safe and effective play. Such policies should cover the level of supervision required by various types of play, scheduling, and the specific types of staff development or training early childhood teachers need to support big body play.

Supervision policies

We know that children need adequate supervision to ensure that all of their activities remain as safe and productive as possible. Insufficient supervision—whether there are not enough adults for the group size and children's developmental levels, or there are lapses in supervision even if enough adults are present—is the major factor in a range of childhood injuries (Morrongiello 2005).

However, according to Peterson and colleagues (1993), "there are currently no commonly accepted standards for what constitutes appropriate supervision for children of any age" (935). The consensus they reached from their research with mothers, child protection service workers, and health care providers is that there are three levels of supervision based on a child's chronological age and the potential hazard of a situation. The three levels of supervision are

- Constant

- Nearly constant

- Close

From birth until children are 4 years old or so, they require *constant* supervision. As the term implies, under constant supervision children are never unsupervised, for any length of time. *Nearly constant* supervision means 0–5 minutes of unsupervised time, and would be appropriate for children as they transition from needing constant supervision to requiring only close supervision.

Once children reach early elementary age (5–8 years old), *close* supervision, or 0–15 minutes of unsupervised time, is often appropriate in low-risk situations, such as an 8-year-old playing near a low-traffic street. Constant supervision might be required for this age group in higher risk

Appropriate, beneficial big body play has smiling children as willing participants, and it occurs in well-planned, safe environments with adequate adult supervision and participation to ensure optimum benefits for children and adults alike.

situations, such as being near a busy street or in a yard with environmental hazards (pools, animals). See the chart "Levels of Supervision for Big Body Play."

Because big body play almost always involves young children's bodies in vigorous contact with other children's bodies, all children under 7

Levels of Supervision for Big Body Play	
Age and type of play	**Level of supervision required**
Infants • crawling • crawling onto another child • pulling up on furniture/equipment and letting go • walking with support • climbing • walking without support	Constant
Toddlers • tumbling • running • chasing • climbing • jumping • tagging	Constant
Preschoolers • tagging • fleeing and chasing • rolling on objects (such as balls) • climbing • jumping from stationary equipment • wrestling	Constant
Preschoolers • running • jumping (broad)	Nearly constant
School age • tagging • fleeing and chasing • rolling on objects (such as balls) • climbing • jumping from stationary equipment	Nearly constant
School age • running • jumping (broad)	Close

or 8 years old should have constant supervision while engaged in most big body play. This is not only to facilitate the play and ensure children's safety but also to provide modeling and coaching for children who may need additional language support.

Because supervision is so important to supporting big body play and implementing it safely and effectively, it will be covered in more detail later in this chapter.

Scheduling policies

Outdoor play should be scheduled to allow children maximum benefit from their big body play. For example, if children have just one brief period of outdoor play per day, sustained vigorous play is less likely to occur. Children tend to have bursts of physical energy but do not maintain high-activity levels for a great length of time, so more frequent play periods support their engagement in rough-and-tumble play (Bower et al. 2008; Cardon et al. 2008). Scheduling longer outdoor periods, as well as indoor physical activity periods, will help children learn to moderate their activity and reach an optimum moderate-to-vigorous activity level. (For indoor big body game suggestions, see Appendix A.)

Consider, also, scheduling opportunities for rough-and-tumble play early in the day. Such play can have a calming effect on children when they engage in it at the beginning of the school day (Scott & Panksepp 2003).

The National Association for Sport and Physical Education (NASPE 2009a) recommends that infants have regular, daily access to movement and large muscle activities—both structured and unstructured. For toddlers, 30 minutes of structured and at least 60 minutes of unstructured physical activity are recommended. Preschoolers should have at least 60 minutes of structured physical activity and at least 60 minutes of unstructured physical activity. NASPE also advocates that toddlers and preschoolers not remain sedentary for more than 60 minutes at a time; it is better to allow some opportunity for active play at least every hour or so. These frequent opportunities for movement lead to better attention and to appropriate rough-and-tumble play. (See "NASPE Guidelines for Physical Activity" in chapter 2.)

Although structured physical education in both preschool and primary school settings leads to the development of important specific motor skills, unstructured play supports sustained, vigorous activity that is also beneficial for children.

Physical education is a program of instruction that teaches children skills and knowledge for maintaining physical fitness and a healthy lifestyle. *Physical activity* is movement of any kind, including movement that occurs during daily activities, recess, and sports or recreational activities. Both are important for children's healthy development (Ballard et al. 2005).

Staff development and training policies

Children are more likely to engage in appropriate rough-and-tumble play when supervised by teachers who have had formal education or training in the importance of play generally and in big body play specifically (Dowda et al. 2004). This means that a key step in making sure that teachers and the curriculum support big body play is to ensure that all teaching staff are taught the importance of vigorous, unstructured physical activity and are trained specifically in how to recognize and facilitate big body play.

However, most teacher resources and staff development opportunities dealing with children's play rarely focus on supporting rough-and-tumble play. A review of child development textbooks typically reveals several pages—and sometimes whole chapters—dedicated to sociodramatic play (such as children's cooperative play in the housekeeping area or construction play in the block area), whereas rough-and-tumble play often receives little more than a cursory mention (Berk 2005; Trawick-Smith 2010).

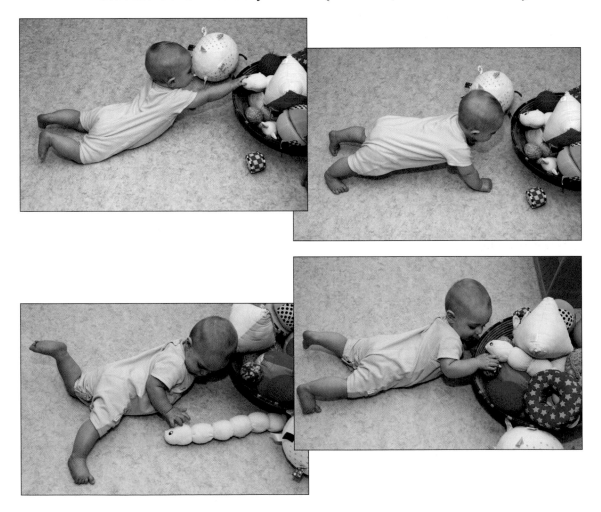

According to Logue & Harvey (2010), 65 percent of teachers would like more training in how to facilitate big body play. Even teachers of very young children recognize a need for this. One teacher noted,

> I have two infant boys in the classroom, one 5 months old and the other 7 months old. The 7-month-old just wants to be all over the 5-month-old. Every time we put the older one down he crawls rapidly to the younger one. To me, this shows the natural desire we all have to get close, to have physical contact with the ones closest to us. It shows that this is a natural part of growing up, and starts very young. We need to find ways of supporting this desire.

To assist staff in understanding and supporting big body play, administrators can include an explanation of the play, its benefits, and the program's policies for it in a staff handbook (see Appendix B for sample policies). Discussing big body play with new and potential staff members, and allowing them an opportunity to speak frankly about their past experiences or concerns, will also demonstrate administrative support for, and expectation of, this play style occurring regularly.

Administrators can provide training—both at the time of employment and ongoing—to help teachers learn about the benefits of big body play and how to ensure that it occurs in a safe environment (see Appendix C for a sample training outline). They can also support teachers by making sure there is adequate staff supervision and by modeling the techniques that support children's learning through big body play.

Sixty-five percent of teachers would like more training in how to facilitate big body play.

Setting up the environment

Because children develop physically, cognitively, socially, and emotionally when playing both indoors and outdoors, their environments should reflect our understanding of this by providing them rich opportunities to

---

Physical Environment Recommendations—NAEYC

NAEYC, through its voluntary program accreditation system and program standards, addresses what quality programs should provide to best support young children's development. Program Standard 9: Physical Environment specifically addresses both the indoor and outdoor environments. For example, NAEYC recommends a minimum of 35 square feet of usable indoor space per child and a minimum of 75 square feet of usable outdoor space per child. This particular standard also requires that children have access to a variety of large motor activities both indoors and outdoors throughout the day. Among these activities are climbing in, on, and over; moving through, around, and under; pushing and pulling. Wherever children are climbing, sufficient ground covering to absorb the shock from any potential fall must be provided.

use their bodies (Curtis & Carter 2005). The way excellent teachers plan environments for young children's big body play demonstrates their understanding of what young children are physically and socially capable of, and the ways children learn best.

When planning for big body play in either an indoor or an outdoor environment, our attention to potential safety hazards must be keen and thoughtful. We want children to play vigorously with their bodies, but we must make it safe for them to do so. National entities including the National Association for the Education of Young Children (NAEYC), the U.S. Consumer Product Safety Commission (CPSC), and ASTM International (formerly known as the American Society for Testing and Materials), as well as the child care licensing agencies in all 50 states and the District of Columbia, set standards and provide guidance for establishing and maintaining safe indoor and outdoor environments in support of young children's play.

For example, in New York, child care environments are mandated to allow—as age and development permits—crawling, standing, walking, and running, and to provide for gross motor play such as climbing, with sufficient teacher supervision to allow children to do so (New York State Office of Children & Family Services 2010). In Texas, classrooms are supported in providing indoor climbing equipment as long as the safety surface underneath will effectively cushion a child's fall (Texas Department of Family and Protective Services 2010). In Illinois, gross motor activities such as climbing and sliding are allowed in areas where all safety surfaces are of a sufficient depth to cushion a fall and have been manufactured specifically to do so (Illinois Department of Children and Family Services 2010).

Furnishings and equipment

The National Health and Safety Performance Standards (AAP, APHA & NRC 2002) provide safety guidance regarding furnishings and equipment. The CPSC's standards also broadly address how to make equipment and furnishings safe for children (see "Top 15 Safety Hazards to Avoid").

When planning outdoor environments to support big body play, be sure to provide plenty of open areas. Children engage in big body play more frequently and do so more appropriately—making or following established rules, taking turns with their peers—when they have access to large, open spaces. Boys, especially, play more actively when more space is available (Cardon et al. 2008; Fry 2005). Playground space that is less structured and has fewer permanently installed, large pieces of equipment (such as climbers) supports children's rough-and-tumble play. Grassy earthen mounds that support rolling and climbing also enhance big body play.

If your playground has large pieces of installed equipment, such as climbers, expect that children will want to use them for leaping and jumping. Make sure each piece of equipment has enough shock-absorbing safety surface beneath it and in the surrounding zone to accommodate this leaping and jumping, and instruct children in how to safely jump—both feet together when landing, and knees bent (KidsHealth 2008).

Ample floor space indoors should also be provided for children's big body play. Open, indoor areas can support a variety of big body activities, such as rolling on large balls, wrestling, and broad jumping. When indoor areas are too cramped or restricted, they hamper children's vigorous play (Finn et al. 2002), and when usable play space is less than 25 square feet per child, children tend to be more aggressive (Pellegrini 1987). For two children to have ample space to support their big body play indoors, at

---

Top 15 Safety Hazards to Avoid

The National Health and Safety Performance Standards list the hazards that the CPSC has identified as most often associated with injury to children:

1. Openings that could entrap a child's head or limbs
2. Elevated surfaces that are inadequately guarded
3. Lack of specified surfacing and fall zones under and around climbable equipment
4. Mismatched size and design of equipment for the intended users
5. Insufficient spacing between equipment
6. Tripping hazards
7. Components that can pinch, sheer, or crush body tissues
8. Equipment that is known to be of a hazardous type (such as large animal swings)
9. Sharp points or corners
10. Splinters
11. Protruding nails, bolts, or other components that could entangle clothing or snag skin
12. Loose, rusty parts
13. Hazardous small parts that may become detached during normal use or reasonably present a choking, aspiration, or ingestion hazard to a child
14. Flaking paint
15. Paint that contains lead or other hazardous materials

Reprinted from AAP, APHA & NRC, *National Health and Safety Performance Standards: Guidelines for Out-of-Home Child Care, 2nd ed.*, 2002, p. 217.

least 50 square feet should be available; four children would require at least 100 square feet.

The arrangement of indoor classroom furnishings and equipment (such as tables, chairs, toy cabinets, block shelves, easels, or sensory tables) should provide ample floor space for children to move around freely. If furniture or equipment is near the open area set aside for rough-and-tumble play, make sure the furnishings have no sharp edges or corners. The furniture should also be firmly anchored to avoid being upturned if a child pushes against it. Ensure that all flooring is skid free, and that safety surfaces are available on the flooring to absorb the shock of any potential impact from a fall. If there are portable climbers in the classroom, they should have shock-absorbing safety surfaces, such as mats or pads, beneath them; carpet or other regular flooring options do not support a child's jump or fall from such equipment.

Some teachers find it helpful to mark off a particular section of the room and dedicate it to big body play. One teacher shared the following as her way of establishing a wrestling zone in her preschool classroom:

> First, clear the area of any furniture or equipment. Next, define the area with a thick, heavy comforter and pillows. After setting up the area, make sure the guidelines for the children's rough play are posted in or near this area.

For infants, the set-up is significantly different. Provide a large open space on the floor for infants to freely explore. If possible, separate this open area from sleeping areas to support infants' active—and sometimes noisy—exploration. Avoid using infant "restraints"—wind-up or battery-operated swings, walkers, bouncers, playpens, and so on. These items interfere with an infant's active exploration and do not provide positive developmental benefits (Greenman et al. 2008). Instead, allow infants plenty of access to unrestrained play on the floor. Provide a variety of safe, mouthable objects in several shapes, colors, and textures. Place the items slightly away from babies to encourage reaching and stretching. Also, provide a variety of large items—inclined hollow blocks, large rubber balls, sturdy tubes, exercise mats—so infants can crawl and roll around, over, and on top of these items.

Join infants on the floor so they can crawl and lay on you. Allow babies to be near each other so that they can play with each other's bodies, being sure to supervise to ensure safe exploration.

Safety surfaces

Young children climb—over each other and onto slides, step stools, block structures, lofts. Children begin climbing in infancy when they are able to pull themselves to a standing position and hold their bodies upright. Al-

Accommodating Big Body Play	
Running	*Indoors*: limit running *Outdoors*: nonskid surface, e.g., recycled rubber, grass (natural or synthetic), poured-in-place; avoid concrete
Skipping and hopping	*Indoors*: nonskid surface *Outdoors*: nonskid, e.g., recycled rubber, grass (natural or synthetic), poured-in-place; avoid concrete
Broad jumping	*Indoors*: nonskid surface *Outdoors*: nonskid, e.g., recycled rubber, grass (natural or synthetic), poured-in-place, sand pit; avoid gravel and concrete
Rolling	*Indoors*: tumbling mats, carpet, bare floor; ensure all surrounding equipment is moved out of the way *Outdoors*: any accepted playground surface except concrete
Jumping from a height	*Indoors*: no jumping from heights *Outdoors*: 6–12 inches of mulch, wood chips, fine sand, and/or fine gravel for heights not to exceed 5 feet

Climbing up and down structures	*Indoors*: Do not allow climbing up and down structures unless
	  1. The structure was designed as a climber and
	  2. There is sufficient shock-absorbing flooring underneath and in the fall zone around the climber (lofts are not included in this category)
	Outdoors: 6–12 inches of mulch, wood chips, fine sand, and/or fine gravel for heights not to exceed 5 feet

Wrestling	*Indoors*: tumbling mats, carpet, bare floor; ensure all surrounding equipment is moved out of the way *Outdoors*: any approved playground surface except concrete; sand is questionable

though children's climbing behavior often concerns adults, climbing helps children develop both upper- and lower-body strength and coordination, balance, body awareness, and self-confidence.

When young children climb, of course, they sometimes jump or fall. Shock-absorbing safety surfaces help protect children's bodies from the impact of landing on the ground. To protect children from serious injury indoors, ensure that all flooring is skid free and that safety surfaces are present over the flooring to absorb the shock of any impact. The chart "Accommodating Big Body Play" lists recommended safety surfaces for a variety of indoor and outdoor play activities.

For outdoor play spaces, the CPSC (2005) recommends the following:

- Make sure surfaces around playground equipment either have at least 12 inches of wood chips, mulch, sand, or pea gravel or are mats made of safety-tested rubber or rubber-like materials.

- Check that protective surfacing extends at least 6 feet in all directions from play equipment. For swings, be sure surfacing extends, in back and front, twice the height of the suspending bar.

- Make sure play structures more than 30 inches high are spaced at least 9 feet apart.

Both indoor and outdoor safety surfaces should be in compliance with CPSC recommendations to prevent life-threatening injuries from falls (see the following chart).

Fall Height in Feet from Which a Life-Threatening Head Injury Would Not Be Expected			
Type of Material	**6" Depth**	**9" Depth**	**12" Depth**
Double-shredded bark mulch	6	10	11
Wood chips	7	10	11
Fine gravel	6	7	10
Fine sand	5	5	9

Reprinted from U.S. Consumer Product Safety Commission, *Home Playground Safety Tips,* http://www.cpsc.gov/CPSCPUB/PUBS/323.html.

Less (Play Equipment) Is More (Big Body Play)

We know that children engage in big body play more frequently and do so more appropriately—making or following established rules and taking turns with their peers—when they have access to large, open spaces. Playground space that is less structured and has fewer permanently installed large pieces of equipment (like climbers) supports children's body play.

At BrightLIFE, A Kid's Campus at Life University in Marietta, Georgia, the outdoor play area supports the children's big body play in these ways (and reflects Life University's philosophy of "the innate wisdom our bodies employ in their own development").

The hills on BrightLIFE's playground support big body play. Children can run up and down or alongside them. They can roll down the hills or bounce balls off of them.

The mounted stumps also support children's big body play. Children can climb up or down them, balance on them, or jump back and forth between them.

The embankment slide allows children to climb up, climb onto, or slide down it without the fear of falling off, as it is mounted in the grassy hill. It offers more independence for very young children and those with special needs. Children also sit on the grassy hill beside the slide and slide down in tandem.

On the sidewalk that winds throughout, children can ride tricycles or play hopscotch or four-square. Children can also bounce balls off of the concrete and each other.

A lot of grassy area supports and promotes wrestling, rolling, running, tagging, twirling, dancing, jumping, skipping, and hopping.

Supporting big body play

The kind of guidance discussed so far in this chapter sets a baseline for avoiding hazards and enabling children to play safely. But following safety guidelines is not the same as setting up the environment to actually *support* big body play. With policies in place, and the environment safe for children's exploration, a third ingredient is needed for effective big body play: teacher support and supervision.

Get active

As mentioned previously, children play more vigorously and more productively when teachers have education or training in the importance of big body play. But it is also true that children play more vigorously and more appropriately when the supervising adults are more active themselves (Bower et al. 2008; Cardon et al. 2008). This is an important insight, as female teachers tend to supervise children's play while standing still or sitting down (Cardon et al.). Not only is supervising active play more challenging if the teacher is standing still or sitting, it also discourages higher activity levels from children. In particular, girls tend to stay in closer proximity to their teachers and to move around less. So girls especially need their teachers to move around, run, climb, throw and catch, and fall down on the ground to encourage them to play this way, too.

> Female teachers historically value development of social skills, and male teachers value development of physical skills. Providing big body play is a way to satisfy the needs of teachers of both genders.

In contrast, male teachers generally tend to value big body play and are more willing to engage in big body play with children (Sandberg et al. 2005), as the following testimonial indicates:

> I'm the only guy in the preschool hall. I've noticed that most of the women I work with aren't real active outside. They usually stand with each other and watch the kids play. My favorite part of working with the kids is all the running around I get to do with them. And they love it! The girls, too—I've noticed—run around with me. But if the women are standing around, the girls will stand around with them. I think they all love the running around, and they love me to chase them.

While a teacher is running around with children, watching children closely as they climb and jump, or being used as a human climber, the children are in close proximity to the teacher, enabling him or her to supervise by both sight and sound. When teachers are standing and chatting on the playground while children play, their big body play may be discouraged, and the lack of appropriate supervision can place children at risk of serious injury (Olsen et al. 2011).

Create rules with children for their play

Preschool and school-age children's big body play is more productive and manageable when simple, clear rules have been established by adults and children together (Flanders et al. 2009). Involving children in creating the rules helps them understand and follow the rules. Rules should be established for rough-and-tumble play as well as for the big body play children engage in with equipment and play materials.

For example, a class might establish the following rules for wrestling: wrestle only while upright on bent knees, and place arms between shoulders and waists, but not around necks or heads. Rules for big body play with equipment may state that sliding and climbing on the slide will occur

on alternate days, or that children can only climb up the slide after checking to make sure no one is sliding down, and that they can jump only from stationary structures and never from swings. There might be a rule that rolling should be done down hills that are fenced in or away from streets or traffic of any kind. Rules for tumbling indoors should include that children always use a mat, and that tumbling cannot be done on a bare floor.

A preschool teacher shared this account of children's rough-and-tumble play and how rules affected it:

> There are a small group of older boys who play pretty rough games with each other. They have gone from wrestling contentedly to wrestling hurtfully, which might be viewed as progressing from playing to fighting, but this could happen in progression of play on any theme. Some of the boys also have been hurt, not seriously, but enough to draw attention to the risks of rough play.
>
> However, instead of taking steps to limit the play, we recognized that this kind of play was natural and important for children, maybe more so for boys, so we tried to formalize it. I brought the group together, and we discussed the rules that we would need to create to make the wrestling games safe. I wrote the rules down, which they decided included the need for a referee to make sure everyone was following the rules. We also designated a space to play the game—on mats, but we could have used big pillows instead. For the rest of the day, and many other days, the kids wrestled in a completely safe and satisfying way, and I was able to document small parts of the experiences to tell families and colleagues about.

According to A Place of Our Own (2007), some rules for wrestling might be:

1. No hitting

2. No pinching

3. Hands below the neck and above the waist

4. STOP as soon as the other person says or signals STOP

5. No rough play while standing—kneeling only

6. Rough play is optional—stop and leave when you want

Write the rules you and the children come up with on white posterboard, and mount them near the designated rough-and-tumble play area. Co-teachers can demonstrate to children what the rules look like when implemented so that children can model the teachers' physical actions. Teachers can also show children how to look for facial gestures and other nonverbal clues that indicate a play partner is uncomfortable or wants to stop the rough play.

Encourage children to tune in to sensations and recognize limits

Children, including infants, benefit from having all kinds of big body experiences, even mildly uncomfortable ones. Naturally, adults must not allow a child to be harmed. But rather than try to halt all uncomfortable physical play, adults should consider how they can use an experience to enhance children's learning in safe ways, even in infancy.

Too often, when infants have an uncomfortable physical interaction—especially if cries result—parents or caregivers stop the play. A more helpful response for encouraging empathy through body play is one that brings the infant's attention to the sensations experienced. For example, continuing the example from chapter 1, caregiver Tasha can help 6-month-old Zoe notice how her movements and interactions with Nate, also 6 months, feel to her body and to his:

> Tasha says to Zoe, "You rolled over. Now you are on Nate. Nate is crying. I don't think he likes how you feel on his arm." After Zoe rolls off, Tasha comments, "Do you hear that Nate stopped crying?"

With older children, as well, teachers can support awareness by coaching children during big body play. A larger child wrestling with a smaller child may not realize that his greater size and strength may affect how long the other child is willing to continue to play. When the smaller child pushes against the chest of the larger boy, indicating that he wants to get up, the larger child may press down even harder. Simply banning the play at this point would deny these children the opportunity to learn how to hold themselves back (self-handicap) so that someone else can participate, as well as the chance to assert themselves.

As you closely supervise children's play, use words to describe some of their nonverbal communication. In the situation above, for example, you might say, "Christopher, Micah is pushing against your chest! He wants to get up!" Help the larger boy to get up if he needs assistance. Point out, "Because you are larger than he is, I think Micah felt uncomfortable with you on top of him." Encourage the smaller child to say these words, too. Help both children problem-solve how to accommodate the size difference by asking, for example, "How else can you wrestle so one of you isn't pinned under the other one?"

In the following observation from a preschool teacher, the children are learning how to recognize each other's cues:

> During indoor gross motor time, two boys were rolling back and forth on a tumbling mat when one boy stopped rolling and straddled the other boy's back. The boy on top reached for and grabbed the other boy's left leg, bending it backwards. The boy yelled out, and the boy on top said, "Count 1-2-3." The boy on the bottom began to cry instead, so the boy on top let

Monitor a child's facial expressions and body language to detect any discomfort in play situations, and then communicate to the other children what you see transpiring.

him go. They then reversed positions, and they continued their play while laughing and waving their arms.

Teachers should explicitly encourage children to recognize their own limits and to be assertive about protecting them by saying, "I've had enough" or "That's too rough." They might teach children to recognize when they are tired or uncomfortable and then provide role-playing activities that enable children to practice using words in a confident but nonaggressive tone that clearly inform their partner that the play needs to end.

Supervise big body play to ensure that everyone benefits

Supervision of big body play may vary with different children. For example, teachers may find that they need to use different support strategies with

boys and girls, socially rejected children, children from varying cultures, and children with varying abilities. With specific supervision, teachers can enrich play experiences for all children.

Optimize supervision for boys' and girls' needs

"Although all [children] have the capacity to learn, not all [children] have an equal capacity to sit quietly and learn" (Logue & Harvey 2010, 33). This statement seems especially true for boys, given their generally higher activity levels and greater tendency to play roughly (Benenson et al. 2008; DiPietro 1981; Humphreys & Smith 1987; Scott & Panksepp 2003). Forty-eight percent of teachers report having stopped or redirected boys' play daily or several times a week; they report stopping girls' play only 29 percent of the time weekly (Logue & Harvey).

Boys' academic performance has lagged for the past 20 years. Perhaps the solution to increasing boys' school success lies not in "fixing" the boys for the program, but in fixing the program for the boys. Providing many opportunities for big body play—with its myriad benefits, including improved language and social skills—could foster boys' short- and long-term academic success. Teachers should supervise boys' big body play from a spot close enough to ensure that it remains safe and appropriate.

Girls need daily, moderate to vigorous unstructured physical activity just as boys do. As we have seen, girls are more likely to participate in active play if their teachers do. Encourage their participation by modeling a vigorous, intense play level yourself—run, throw, twirl, skip, hop—and by stepping back a foot or two when they are playing among themselves. Remain close enough to supervise their play, but far enough that they will feel more comfortable playing this way (Bower et al. 2008).

Support children who are socially rejected

Rough-and-tumble play is 25 times more likely to become aggression or real fighting when a child who has experienced social rejection is one of the participants (Schafer & Smith 1996; Smith et al. 2004). This makes adequate supervision critical. If the play escalates into fighting, it is usually due to (1) a child's lack of communication skills or (2) a child's lack of turn-taking skills.

Children who are socially rejected may lack the communication skills—both verbal and nonverbal—needed to interpret spoken words as well as body signals and body language, which makes rough-and-tumble play difficult for them. A preschool teacher shared the following story of how an episode of play-fighting escalated when one boy did not understand what was happening in the other boys' play:

Moderate physical activity might be rolling around on a ball, playing variations of tag, or climbing up a slide and sliding down. **Vigorous activity** might be playing chase, climbing and jumping, or climbing up a hill and rolling down.

> Four boys began to build something with the magnetic blocks. One boy took some of the blocks from one of the other boys, and then it became a game of getting on top of each other to try to take the blocks back. They were laughing and smiling. Then, another boy came up, took a block, and hit one of the children. The boys stopped laughing—they looked angry— and they began to go at it with the new boy. They were all upset then.

In this scenario, the child who walked up and hit another child with a block misread the facial expressions of the children and the intentions of their play. He perceived that their play-fighting was real fighting, and he probably thought it was appropriate to join in by taking a block and hitting someone. He did not recognize the difference between their rolling around and playing at taking blocks from each other and his hitting and taking blocks by force.

Children who are socially rejected may feel challenged or threatened by another child's movement or action. They may misinterpret a child's sudden turn in their direction as an attack, or they may feel a slight push from a child trying to get down a walkway as a slap and reciprocate by slapping back. A teacher related the following:

> Thomas was a 4-year-old in our preK program. One day while he was walking through the classroom, another 4-year-old was rolling around on the floor. The child had both legs straight up in the air and was rolling side to side. One of his feet hit Thomas's leg as he walked by.
>
> Thomas stopped and lunged at the boy and began hitting him. I quickly intervened. I stopped Thomas from hitting, and explained that the boy hadn't been kicking Thomas—he was just rolling around on the floor. I showed Thomas how to walk around the boy. Later that day when Thomas was in the block area, I encouraged him to lie on the floor and wave his legs in the air.

Children who are socially rejected may also lack the social skill of turn taking (reciprocity). They often do not understand that play involves give-and-take, and that they will also get a turn at the action or movement.

Teachers should have a special focus on facilitating and supporting big body play for children who are socially awkward. Encourage them to engage in big body play with others, and encourage others to play with them so they can build their language and social skills. When supervising a child who is socially rejected, however, remain closer than you would to a child who navigates play well.

Intervene if you see that a socially rejected child may be misunderstanding other children's cues or their turn taking. For example, if a child misreads a tag as a slap, stop the play, but only long enough to say, "That was a tag. It wasn't meant to hurt you. You'll get to tag someone with your hand when it's your turn." Provide children with tips on reading others' behavior ("See how Ryan and Jameson are both smiling as they wrestle? They must be having fun!"). Give children chances to role-play, helping them learn to interpret events as neutral or friendly rather than aggressive, and practicing ways to stop play-fighting with words rather than hitting when they want the play to end.

Here are some additional tools:

- Coaching ("Lauren, try tagging more gently when it's your turn. Like this . . . see how gentle that feels? Tagging too hard can hurt.")

- Helping the child reflect on cues and responses ("Look, Jordan! Alex's face is getting red! I think you need to get off of him for a minute so he can catch his breath.")

- Explaining and modeling sharing and reciprocity ("Julie, you'll get to jump down next—right after Elizabeth jumps down.")

Such tools will help children who are socially rejected remain in the play, and ultimately increase their language and social competence. Your intervention should not stop the play permanently; instead, it should help clarify the child's understanding of the play so that it can continue.

When supervising a child who is socially rejected, remain closer than you would to a child who navigates play well.

Without close supervision, modeling, mentoring, and guiding, the rough-and-tumble play of children with weak social skills can quickly get out of hand. But with support, this play will help them develop signal decoding skills, reciprocity or turn-taking skills, and verbal communication. These skills will enable them to participate effectively, not only in this type of play but in all play with their peers.

If you are concerned about children in your classroom exhibiting aggression, Malloy & McMurray-Schwarz (2004) recommend the following strategies:

- Identify, first, whether or not the behavior really is aggression (see chapter 1 for the three main differences between play-fighting and real fighting).

- Talk to families about limiting violent television programs and toys.

- Talk with the children about their fighting and how it affects their peers.

- Restructure peer groups so socially rejected children have more socially competent children to model appropriate behaviors for them.

- Guide and support conflict resolution.

- Avoid banning play. Instead, facilitate continued engagement with open-ended props and your constant supervision.

Accommodate cultural differences in play

When supervising groups with culturally diverse children, be mindful that children's big body play will reflect their individual cultural experiences. For example, a child who has experienced little or no boisterous physical activity will probably be uncomfortable with such play at first, preferring more mild physical contact with other children. An aunt of a 6-year-old girl shared this:

> Renee is an only child—and a girl—and she didn't have much big, physical play as an infant or toddler. In my culture, children play very gently with each other. So, now when she comes to visit her cousins in the U.S.—my boys—they want to rough-and-tumble with her, and she doesn't know how to respond. She cries and runs away. I try to help by telling them to be gentle with her—hug her instead of grabbing her to wrestle, and throw the ball gently to her instead of throwing it at her. I hope she will one day enjoy playing with the boys, but for right now she's afraid of them and how rough they are.

Monitor a child's facial expressions and body language to detect any discomfort in play situations, and then communicate to the other children what you see transpiring. Coaching a child on taking turns and assisting him or her with decoding other children's signals will also help the child feel more comfortable with the play.

Support children of varying abilities

For children with disabilities or developmental delays, the intensity of big body play is almost always lower than for typically developing children. Children with disabilities tend to play more passively. They watch more and initiate less. However, children with special needs often have the same preferences for active play and the same developmental need for physical challenges (Case-Smith & Kuhaneck 2008; Prellwitz & Skar 2007). Make sure opportunities for big body play are available for *all* children by providing active supervision and by supporting each child's attempts to use his or her body in new and challenging ways.

For a typically developing child who is climbing up, over, and back down a 6-foot rope ladder, supervision may consist of being close enough to assist with body lifting and with the child's balance as the child navigates the rope ladder. For a child with a disability or delay wishing to negotiate the same ladder, an appropriate physical challenge may be getting to the rope ladder and putting a hand or a foot on it. The supervision required here is that the teacher support the child's mobility, strength, and balance as he moves his body to the rope ladder and as he lifts his body to it.

Determining what constitutes an appropriate challenge for a child with a developmental disability or delay, and knowing how to approach the

All children, whatever their physical abilities and limitations, need physical challenge from a playground: the opportunity to literally *reach new heights* and *run wild*. They need the stimulus of risk; they need choices so that they can determine the excitement and challenge they are ready for (Greenman 2007, 290–91).

challenge, requires the teacher to be very aware of the child's capabilities and what assistance is needed. The safety information presented earlier in this chapter is particularly important when setting up the environment to include children with special needs.

Communicating and collaborating with families

Children thrive in early childhood programs when administrators, teachers, and family members work together in partnership (Keyser 2006). For children to feel supported in their big body play, this partnership is crucial. Young children are better positioned to reap the benefits of developmentally appropriate practices in play when these practices are consistently used both at home and at school. In the following example, a teacher noted how support from both staff and parents for two children's rough-and-tumble play led to rich play experiences and friendship for the children:

> One year, we had two older boys in our 3-year-old class because of a need for developmental and language support. They immediately bonded and would engage in social play with each other while the younger 3s were still

at parallel play and associative play. They would play pirates, bad guys, and space men, chasing each other and roughhousing using sticks as weapons. They demonstrated joy in their play and really were a duo, with frequent play dates outside of class. The parents were grateful that we let them play this way and did not try to restrain them.

Teachers can partner with parents in supporting big body play by explaining its use and benefits and by encouraging parents to engage in it with their children at home.

Helping parents understand big body play in the classroom

Along with their other fears about rough-and-tumble play, teachers may be concerned about parents' reactions to their children engaging in this play. A teacher in a child care program noted,

> Some parents already may not understand that children learn through play. If these parents were to come upon their child engaging in rough-and-tumble play, it would probably look to them like their child is involved in a fight. They would surely not understand that their child is learning social behavior through this type of play.

In industrialized countries, rough-and-tumble play is probably the most commonly used play style between parents and their children after the children are at least 2 years old (Paquette et al. 2003).

If big body play is an essential component in your program, make sure the families you serve are aware of this and understand why you have chosen to facilitate it. The best time to communicate program components to families is at the time of initial interest in your program or at events that may precede the first day of school, such as an open house. You can communicate your support for big body play in a variety of ways:

- Include a policy on big body play—and how it is supported and supervised in your program or school—in your family handbook (see Appendix B for a sample policy).

- Send a letter to families that explains big body play and its many benefits (see Appendix D for a sample letter).

- Visually demonstrate children engaging in big body play by taking photographs similar to the ones in this book and displaying them in newsletters; documentation panels (see example in Appendix E); promotional literature, such as brochures and flyers; and bulletin boards at entryways.

Supportive big body play at home

Just as teachers' views on rough-and-tumble play vary, so do parents'. Not all find it unacceptable. Some mothers stated in interviews that such play is empowering for girls and that they appreciated how strong this play style made girls feel (*Rough and tumble play*, 2008). A mother of three who supports rough-and-tumble play said,

> I was unaware that other parents might see rough-and-tumble play as a dangerous childhood game. Young children should get the opportunity to play roughly with each other. Such games are harmless as long as they are having fun and the play is helping them develop mentally and socially.

Although big body play generally involves physically interactive play between children, children benefit when parents get involved in their play. Social skills, especially, seem enhanced when parents roughhouse with their young children. For example, when fathers participate in young children's big body play by smiling and by being responsive and emotionally attuned to their children, the children's social and language skills improve (Shannon et al. 2002). And although boys are more likely to play roughly with a parent than girls are, girls enjoy playing this way with a parent, too (Paquette et al. 2003).

There are other tangible benefits to parent-child rough-and-tumble play. When parents set limits and maintain control over the play, children tend to demonstrate lower levels of physically aggressive behaviors in their everyday lives (Flanders et al. 2009). For example, a father may be wrestling with a 3-year-old child. Dad occasionally lets the 3-year-old win the wrestling match, but he does not let the child hit him repeatedly in excitement after winning. With this parent's sensitivity to his child's need to dominate in rough play, and the modeling of physically interactive behaviors that are acceptable (wrestling) and that are not (hitting), the child is more likely to engage in rough-and-tumble play appropriately and not confuse it with actual fighting.

✳   ✳   ✳

Research demonstrates convincingly that there is physical, social, emotional, and cognitive value in children's big body play. As early childhood education professionals, we are entrusted with the responsibility of providing children with what best serves their developmental needs—and also the need of each child to have the very best possible childhood. Big body play's success is "a measure of the children's social well-being and is marked by the ability of children to . . . cooperate, to lead, and to follow" (Burdette & Whitaker 2005, 48). These abilities—cooperating, leading, and following—will serve children well, lifelong.

Frequently Asked Questions about Big Body Play

What do I do if a child accidentally gets hurt during rough-and-tumble play?

When children are playing roughly, accidents can happen—just as they can when children are playing with blocks, riding tricycles, or simply walking through the classroom. Respond to these accidents in the same way you would to any accident that occurs during play: Make sure the area is safe, go immediately to the injured child, and apply first aid. If the child is seriously injured, call your emergency help line or 911. Notify administration and the child's parent or guardian immediately anytime an accident requires first aid.

An accident during big body play may raise concerns about the wisdom of allowing children to play this way, particularly if concern has been expressed before. Once you have attended to the child's injuries, reflect on the play to see if the accident could have been prevented, perhaps with more supervision or by helping children better understand and respond to verbal and nonverbal cues during the play. Reassure parents and administrators that the children's rough-and-tumble play is safe and is being adequately supervised.

Is it okay to let children climb up the slide, or slide down it on their stomachs? They all want to do this, but my principal said it is too dangerous.

Climbing up a slide is no more dangerous than sliding down it as long as multiple children are not climbing up and sliding down simultaneously. One teacher puts arrows on the slide so children will know whether it is okay to

75

climb up or just to slide down on that particular day. Having a system that clearly communicates your expectations to children helps them be successful and safe. Remember that children should not be sliding down *or* climbing up slides without sufficient ground cover underneath and around the fall zone.

Sliding down a slide *head first*, however, presents a hazard. Children could hit the ground with their head or hand, and the possibility of a head or hand injury outweighs any potential benefit from this particular activity. Even baseball players are taught to try not to slide in to base head or hand first, because it is just too dangerous.

What should I do if the kids are smiling and laughing, but jabbing at each other's genitals—should I let them play this way, or stop it?

The same rule of thumb that guides so much of best practice with young children also applies to their rough-and-tumble play. Because children are learning through their play, our job is to help sustain the play in a positive manner as long as possible. If children are playing in ways you know could be dangerous for their bodies, like jabbing eyes or genitals, stop the play, but just long enough to bring the possible danger to their attention. You might say, "Punching and jabbing at each other's private parts can hurt them. I can't let you do that. You can keep wrestling, but remember that the rule is no hands below the belt or above the shoulders." Constantly supervise to make sure children follow the rules. If they are unable to do so, redirect their play temporarily, and then offer them another chance to play appropriately.

I just can't get comfortable with the idea of letting children in my care play so roughly—it just looks too dangerous. Will it really hurt them if I don't allow it?

Denying a child the opportunity to play in a particular way should not cause permanent developmental harm. Because this play style supports so much of a child's development, however, having opportunities to play this way can be very valuable. Consider the types of big body play with which you *could* feel comfortable. Maybe you're not ready to encourage wrestling bouts, but you might feel comfortable with encouraging and supporting children to roll down a grassy incline on your playground, or broad jump into a sand pit. Stretching our own comfort zones and skills takes time, just as it does for children. Thinking about different ways children might engage in this play, and discussing it with your colleagues, is a good place to start.

For most children, I can see how rough-and-tumble play is fine, and even beneficial, but there is a boy in my class who always ends up in a fight before recess is over. For his own (and others') protection, isn't it better to keep him away from play-fighting and rough games?

You absolutely must protect all the children in your class. However, denying a child who struggles with rough-and-tumble play the chance to participate in it denies him the chance to develop the very skills he probably lacks. Supervise the play constantly when any children are playing this way, but pay specific attention when a struggling child is involved. This child needs you to intervene when you first observe a loss of control—not to stop the play permanently, but to stop it long enough to give the child the tools he needs to keep playing without fighting. Chapter 3 discusses some specific tools you can use, such as coaching, helping children read cues, and modeling.

It makes me really nervous when Anderson plays with Claire. They are both 2½, but he is much heavier and bigger than she is. They have developed this game that they both seem to love where they hug each other and try to pick each other up, and then they fall over laughing and roll around on each other. Isn't this too dangerous for them?

Picking up an equivalent amount of one's body weight does seem scary. The other parts of their play, however—hugging, squeezing, falling over, and rolling around—are not scary. Think of some rules you could introduce that might make this play safer. Perhaps the children have to be kneeling to play this way—no standing and lifting from the ground. They can get the same benefit and enjoyment if they kneel and then hug, squeeze, fall to the ground, and roll over on each other. Tumbling mats will support this play and add further safety—just make sure the furniture is out of the way.

I understand that jumping is a part of big body play and is good for children, but is all jumping okay? Should I let kids jump down from the climber and from the top of the playhouse? And how about jumping from swings?

Jumping *is* good for children. When children are jumping, however, keep two things in mind: (1) Children should not be allowed to jump from a height greater than their own height (e.g., a 3-foot-tall child should not jump down from a height greater than 3 feet), and (2) children should know how to land properly when jumping. Their knees should be slightly bent and they should land on both feet at the same time. The ground cover beneath and around your climbing structures will help cushion the impact from jumping as long as you have enough ground cover and the children land properly.

Jumping from swings, however, is hazardous for many reasons and should be avoided. When a child jumps from a swing, her body is launched outward and then downward and is thrown with the full force of the swinging motion. This makes the impact to the child's body when landing greater and potentially too dangerous. It is also difficult to land properly when jumping from a moving object, and so the risk of joint injury is greater. Bottom line: Encourage broad jumping and jumping down from fixed, acceptable heights onto shock-absorbing surfaces, but supervise to prevent jumping from swings.

I teach in an elementary school. How can I show that big body play is helping children meet our state standards?

Think of a particular big body activity that children might engage in—for example, wrestling. At first glance, wrestling may not seem to support many state standards for students. But let's look at first grade in a Georgia elementary school. Here are some of the state standards for first-graders:

- Demonstration of both speaking and listening skills (e.g., following a three-part direction)
- Beginning to understand the principles of writing
- Measuring attributes of concrete objects
- Understanding the measurement of time
- Demonstrating competency in motor skills and movement patterns needed to perform a variety of activities

A supervised wrestling match can help first-graders develop mastery of these standards. For example, you could involve students in creating the wrestling ring, using rulers and tape measures to determine the size. Have students develop the rules for the game and write them down on posterboard. Appoint a timekeeper to watch the clock and let participants know when the bout is over.

My director said we will lose our NAEYC accreditation if I let the kids roughhouse. Does NAEYC support this kind of play?

For more than 25 years, NAEYC has offered a national, voluntary accreditation system to set professional standards for early childhood education programs, and to help families identify high-quality programs. Teachers in NAEYC-accredited programs are encouraged to support children in their efforts to make friends, develop physical and emotional self-regulation, resolve conflicts, develop strong language skills, and build strong, healthy bodies. Implemented safely and properly supervised, big body play provides these developmental benefits to children.

How can I help a child learn to play this way when the child doesn't want to or doesn't seem to enjoy it?

As with any learning opportunity a child may not enjoy or feel comfortable with, continuing to offer occasions to try it can be beneficial. A child who does not like rolling on the ground today may find he enjoys it a few weeks later. Perhaps it is not the body play the child doesn't enjoy but the high levels of physical contact with other children. Make sure children have a wide variety of big body play opportunities available—both solitary ones such as broad jumping in a sand pit and collaborative ones such as sack races—so that individual needs and preferences can be met.

If a child seems interested in a certain type of play but hesitant to get involved, help the child find a "safe" way to participate, such as being the timekeeper for wrestling matches. This allows the child to be part of the play in a nonthreatening way, and the child can observe the play and become familiar with it. In time, the child might choose to join the play more directly. In short, do not force big body play on a child, but offer opportunities for engagement, and encourage and model the play.

I have several children with special needs in my program. Should I encourage them in big body play? How do I help the other children play without hurting them?

Children with physical disabilities or developmental delays have the same need and desire to play that their typically developing peers do. Working closely with any support staff that children with special needs may have can help ensure that the environment and activities are appropriate for their individual needs and allow for their full participation. Here are a couple of examples of what supporting big body play with children with special needs might look like:

> Christopher is 11 months old and wears leg braces. To support his big body play in the classroom, his teachers make sure he has a lot of open space in which to crawl, along with big balls and soft climbing pieces nearby so he can crawl to, on, and around them. When he crawls on top of another child—or when another child crawls on top of him—a teacher helps the children get off each other and expresses for the children their discomfort ("Christopher, Leah cried when you crawled on top of her. I'm going to help you crawl off her now").

> Jake is a 3-year-old with autism. Although he tries to use speech to communicate, he cannot communicate effectively with his peers or his teachers. His teachers closely supervise him when he engages in big body play with the other children. They also model signals and other means of nonverbal communication for him and for the other children, such as how to express "Come here" and "Stop" using hands and fingers.

All children require close supervision, as well as coaching and modeling, during big body play. Recognizing that children's varying physical and verbal abilities can make big body play even more challenging reminds us how important it is to provide active supervision and model language and nonverbal cues.

Appendix

This Appendix contains resources to support efforts to provide a positive environment for children's big body play in early childhood programs.

Appendix A contains several traditional finger plays that can be adapted for big body play to encourage children to move vigorously and interactively.

Appendix B contains sample policy language on big body play that can be adapted for both family and staff handbooks. The sample policies cover programs serving children birth to age 3 and preschool/school-age programs. This material is meant only as a starting point for communicating policy; individual policies must be tailored to reflect your program's specific needs and to comply with all federal, state, and local laws and regulations.

A general outline for training staff on rough-and-tumble play is found in **Appendix C. Appendix D** offers a sample family letter regarding big body play. **Appendix E** contains a sample documentation panel to help parents and others understand what children learn from a specific big body play experience.

Turning Finger Plays into Big Body Games

A typical child development curriculum includes finger plays—rhymes and songs with accompanying finger and hand movements that allow children to develop both literacy and fine motor skills. To support children's big body play, think of turning these finger and hand movements into arm, leg, and whole-body movements. You can also encourage children to develop their own body movements to act out familiar finger plays.

When leading these games indoors, make sure the environment is free from surrounding objects and has a skid-proof floor covering and, if possible, some type of tumbling mat or padding. Encourage the children to move vigorously and interactively.

Five Little Bees

One little bee blew and flew
  (Child holds arms out like wings and runs around)
He met a friend, and that made two
  (Child joins first child and both children hold arms out like wings and run around)
Two little bees, busy as could be
  (Both children run around like bees)
Along came another, and that made three
  (Three children run around like bees)
Three little bees, wanted one more
Found one soon, and that made four
  (Fourth child joins and all four run around like bees)
Four little bees, going to the hive
Spied their little brother/sister, and that made five
  (Fifth child joins and all five run around like bees)
Five little bees, working every hour
Buzz away, bees, and find another flower
  (All the bees run around like bees)

Four Baby Turtles

One baby turtle alone and new
  (Child crawls around on the floor)
Finds a friend and then there are two
  (Child crawls on floor toward another child)
Two baby turtles crawl down to the sea
  (Two children crawl around on the floor)
They find another and then there were three
  (Two children crawl on floor toward another child and join her/him)
Three baby turtles crawl along the shore
  (Three children crawl around on the floor)
They find another and then there were four
  (Three children crawl toward another child and join her/him)
Four baby turtles go for a dive
  (Each child makes vigorous swimming motions with arms and legs)
Up swims another and then there are five
  (Four children "swim" on floor toward another child and join him/her)

The Eensy Weensy Spider

The eensy weensy spider crawled up the water spout
  (Children crawl across the floor)
Down came the rain and washed the spider out
  (Children roll back across the floor in the opposite direction)
Up came the sun and dried up all the rain
  (Children wave arms and legs back and forth vigorously while lying on their backs)
And the eensy weensy spider crawled up the spout again
  (Children crawl across the floor)

Rock-a-Bye Baby

Rock-a-bye baby on the treetop
  (Rock and sway body back and forth)
When the wind blows, the cradle will rock
  (Rock and sway more vigorously)
When the bough breaks, the cradle will fall
  (Bend from the waist toward the ground, fall to the ground)
And down will come baby, cradle and all
  (Roll around on the ground)

Here We Go

Here we go up, up, up,
(Stand and jump up and down)
Here we go down, down, down
(Fall down to the floor/ground)
Here we go forward
(Run forward)
Here we go backward
(Run backward)
Here we go round, round, round
(Run around in circles)

Five Little Pumpkins

Five little pumpkins sitting on a gate
(Children squat up and down)
The first one said, "Oh, my! It's getting late!"
(Children jump up from squatting position and jump up and down)
The second one said, "There's a chill in the air."
(Children shiver and shake vigorously)
The third one said, "But I don't care!"
(Children throw arms out to sides and sway back and forth)
The fourth one said, "I'm ready for some fun!"
(Children dance around in circles)
The fifth one said, "Let's run and run and run!"
(Children run around)
"Woooooooo" went the wind and out went the lights
(Children drop to the ground)
And the five little pumpkins rolled out of sight
(Children roll around on the floor)

I'm a Little Popcorn

I'm a little popcorn in a pot
(Children huddle closely together on the rug)
Heat me up and watch me pop
(Children, one at a time, jump up from the rug and jump around)
When the noise stops, I am all done
(Children freeze in position)
Popping corn is so much fun
(Children continue vigorously jumping around)

The Train

Choo, choo, choo
(Children crawl around the floor on hands and knees)
The train runs down the track
(Children now follow each other while crawling on their hands and knees)
Choo, choo, choo
(Children crawl around in different directions)
And then it runs right back
(Children follow each other while crawling on their hands and knees)

Little Fishes

Many little fishes, side by side
(Children lay side by side on the floor)
Swim through the water, swim through the tide
(Children make vigorous swimming motions with their hands and feet)
They don't need a motor, and they don't need a sail
(Children swim more vigorously with arms and legs)
They just wiggle their fins, and wiggle their tails
(Children wiggle their whole bodies vigorously)

Many Little Blackbirds

Many little blackbirds sitting on the hill
(Children squat down and then bounce up and down)
Some named Jack,
(Some of the children jump up)
And some named Jill
(The rest of the children jump up)
Fly away, Jack!
(Some of the children run around, flapping their arms in a flying motion)
Fly away, Jill!
(The rest of the children run around, flapping their arms in a flying motion)
Come back, Jack!
(Some of the children run back to the teacher)
Come back, Jill!
(The rest of the children run back to the teacher)

Many thanks to all of my ECE 1012 Curriculum Development students for helping me develop these games and try them out.

Sample Handbook Policies for Big Body Play

Big body play for children birth–age 3

Here at [*name of program*], we believe in the value of exuberant, boisterous, rough-and-tumble play to a child's overall development. This vigorous body play allows very young children opportunities to learn about their bodies and how to regulate them, as well as how to begin to relate to other children and show concern for them. Big body play also contributes to infants' and toddlers' physical development because it is so vigorous and because children—since they enjoy it so much—tend to engage in it for an extended amount of time.

To support the use of big body play, we do the following:

- Provide training to all staff on the importance of big body play for infants and toddlers and how to supervise it
- Prepare both indoor and outdoor environments for this play style
- Provide infants ample amounts of floor time to support their big body play; limit the use of wind-up swings, bouncers, jumpers, playpens, and other restrictive equipment so infants can freely move and actively explore their environment
- When applicable, establish classroom and playground rules to keep children safe and help them know what to expect
- Encourage staff to use big body games with the children
- Supervise children's play constantly, which means ensuring an adult is watching and listening at all times
- Model appropriate play and assist children so that they are able to play comfortably with each other in this way

The following indoor and outdoor environmental features of our program support big body play:

- At least 50 square feet of open indoor play space per child, free from furniture and equipment so that younger children can roll, turn over, and crawl, and so that older children can tumble
- At least 100 square feet of open outdoor play space per child, free from fixed equipment so that children can crawl, run, roll, jump, twirl, fall down, and chase
- Safety surfaces indoors under and around climbers and furniture that children might use as climbers (a loveseat, for example)
- Safety surfaces outdoors under and around right-sized climbers, slides, and elevated surfaces from which children might jump

Big body play for preschool and school-age children

Here at [*name of school or program*], we believe in the value of exuberant, boisterous, rough-and-tumble play to a child's overall development. This vigorous body play allows children opportunities to use language—both verbal and nonverbal—and learn how to negotiate, take turns, wait, compromise, sometimes dominate and sometimes hold back, and make and follow rules. They are learning about cause and effect and developing empathy. Big body play also supports optimum physical development because it is so vigorous and because children—since they enjoy it so much—tend to engage in it for an extended amount of time.

To support the use of big body play, we do the following:

- Provide training to all staff on the importance of big body play and how to supervise it

- Prepare both indoor and outdoor environments for this play style

- Establish classroom and playground rules with the children to keep them safe and help them know what to expect

- Encourage staff to use big body games with the children

- Supervise the play constantly, which means ensuring an adult is watching and listening at all times

- Model appropriate play; coach children as they play so that they are able to interact comfortably with each other in this way

The following indoor and outdoor environmental features of our program support big body play:

- At least 50 square feet of usable indoor play space per child, free from furniture and equipment so that children can tumble and wrestle (for example, a wrestling area for two children would consist of at least 100 square feet with no furnishings in the area)

- At least 100 square feet of usable outdoor play space per child, free from fixed equipment so that children can run, jump, tag, roll, wrestle, twirl, fall down, and chase each other (for example, a group of six children playing tag would have at least 600 square feet in which to play)

- Safety surfaces indoors under and around climbers, and furniture that children might use as climbers (a loveseat, for example)

- Safety surfaces outdoors under and around climbers, slides, balance beams, and other elevated surfaces from which children might jump

Training Staff on Rough-and-Tumble Play

Goal

To increase understanding about appropriate rough-and-tumble play and how to encourage and support it.

Objectives

1. To learn the differences between hurtful, aggressive actions and appropriate rough-and-tumble play

2. To understand the positive effects appropriate rough-and-tumble play has on young children's development

3. To discover ways to encourage and supervise appropriate rough-and-tumble play for optimum developmental benefits

Key Points

• Humans are not the only species drawn to rough-and-tumble play; all animal young play roughly with their own and others' bodies.

• Rough-and-tumble play rarely leads to serious injury.

• There are three main differences between inappropriate real fighting and appropriate rough-and-tumble play:

  1. In real fighting, one or all children are frowning or crying. In rough-and-tumble play, children are laughing and smiling.

  2. In real fighting, one child is clearly dominating another child or children and keeping them in the situation against their will. In rough-and-tumble play, all children are willing participants.

  3. In real fighting, one child or children run away as soon as possible. In rough-and-tumble play, children sustain the play and willingly return for more.

• Appropriate rough-and-tumble play supports young children's social-emotional, cognitive, and physical development.

• Rough-and-tumble play requires adult supervision as well as environments that support it.

Reflection Questions

- Think back on your own childhood: in what ways did you play roughly with your and others' bodies?
- Think of times you've seen young children playing roughly:
    1. What were their facial expressions?
    2. Did the children appear to be participating willingly?
    3. Did the children continue playing, or did they flee?

Exercise

- Think about the times you've seen young children playing roughly:
    1. Based on the three criteria used to determine whether play is appropriate rough-and-tumble play or inappropriate real fighting, what do you think each situation was?
    2. For each one you determine was appropriate rough-and-tumble play, what could you have done as the teacher to further support it?
    3. For each one you determine was real fighting, what could you have done as the teacher to stop the fighting and get the appropriate rough-and-tumble play back on track?

Sample Letter for Families

Dear Family Members,

You probably remember playing active games like Tag or King of the Hill when you were a child, or playing in other very vigorous and rowdy ways. We believe that children need to play in these ways. We sometimes call this big body play.

We also believe that taking some risks will help children grow physically, emotionally, socially, and cognitively. Big body play is one of the ways we encourage children to take risks. While we believe that risk is necessary, your child's safety and well-being are our greatest concerns. We are sending you this letter so that you will know the ways we supervise and support big body play, and why we believe this play style is so important to your child's development.

If your child is an infant, our teaching staff will play games like "horsey" while bouncing your baby on a knee or an ankle. We will give your baby plenty of time on the floor to learn about his or her body and how it moves. Babies who are moving around will have opportunities to roll into/onto and climb off of other babies who are moving around. We will also help your baby learn how his or her body movements affect another baby's comfort.

Big body play will help your toddler learn to control his or her movements. We will play movement games with your toddler, like Eensy Weensy Spider but with arms and legs instead of just fingers. We will have lots of outdoor time so your child can enjoy moving in whatever ways he or she wants to. Your toddler may swing arms with a friend or fall down and roll around while dancing to music or playing next to other toddlers.

Your preschooler may make up running and chasing games with friends or play many variations of Tag. He or she will wrestle, tumble, roll down hills and on flat surfaces, and jump across grass or pavement. Your child might play alone by jumping off climbers onto a safety surface.

We support this play style because it provides so many benefits for your child. When children play vigorously and sometimes roughly, they are learning how to use language and how to take turns, how to give in a little bit, how to sometimes dominate and sometimes hold back, and how to make and follow rules. They are learning about cause and effect, and they are learning how to understand how other children feel.

Our staff are trained to consistently monitor children during big body play. In infant and toddler groups, they play with children to show them appropriate physical contact and to name the emotions they might be feeling. In preschool groups, they help children establish rules for their games and closely watch the play to keep it enjoyable for everyone. In classrooms as well as on the playground, floor or ground covering keeps children safe, and equipment supports their big body play.

Thank you for choosing our program for your child. We want to continue to earn your trust by providing the best possible care and education.

Sincerely,

Sample Documentation Panel

Documentation panels are a tool early childhood educators can use to show families, colleagues, administrators, and others what children are learning. A documentation panel, such as the one shown below, uses photographs and descriptions to depict a particular experience and what children learned from it. It is an ideal way to communicate the learning that occurs as part of children's big body play.

When creating a documentation panel, use close-ups of photographs so readers can see the action **A**. Describe what is happening in each

photograph **B**, using some of the children's own statements made during or about the play. To communicate how the experience helped children move toward standards mastery, refer to your state standards **C** and then tell how the experience related to those standards **D**. For example, in the "Learning Through Wrestling" panel shown here, readers can see that wrestling allowed these two boys to practice communicating both verbally and nonverbally and recognizing their own feelings and those of others.

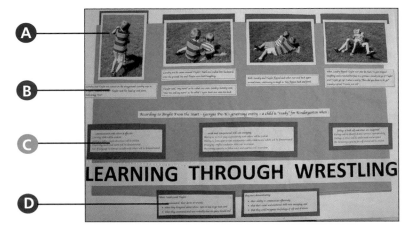

Landry and Taylor are outside on the playground.
Landry says to Taylor, "Wanna wrestle?"
Taylor nods, indicating, "Yes!"

Landry puts his arms around Taylor's back and pulls him backward onto the ground. He and Taylor are both laughing.

Both Landry and Taylor flip each other over several times, continuing to laugh.

When Landry flips Taylor over onto his back, Taylor stops laughing and scrunches his face into a grimace. Landry lets go of Taylor, and Taylor gets up. The teacher asks Landry, "How did you know to let go?" Landry replies, "I could just tell."

According to Bright from the Start: Georgia Department of Early Care and Learning—Georgia's Pre-K governing entity—a child is ready for kindergarten when

. . . social and interpersonal skills are emerging

- Ability to work or play cooperatively with others will be evident.
- Ability to form appropriate relationships with children and adults will be demonstrated.
- Emerging conflict-resolution skills will be evident.
- Increasing capacity to follow rules and routines will be evident.

. . . communication with others is effective

- Listening skills will be evident.
- Ability to follow simple directions will be evident.
- Expressing needs and wants will be demonstrated.
- Use of language to interact socially with others will be demonstrated.

. . . feelings of both self and others are recognized

- Feelings will be identified and expressed appropriately.
- Feelings of others will be understood and accepted.
- An increasing capacity for self-control will be evident.

When Landry and Taylor

- Communicated their desire to wrestle
- Disagreed about whose turn it was to go next
- Communicated nonverbally that the play should end

They were demonstrating

- That they could recognize the feelings of themselves and others
- That their social and interpersonal skills were emerging
- That they could communicate effectively with others

References

A Place of Our Own. 2007. *Rough play area.* Online: http://aplaceofourown.org/activity.php?id=492.

Alhassan, S., J.R. Sirard & T.N. Robinson. 2007. The effects of increasing outdoor play time on physical activity in Latino preschool children. *International Journal of Pediatric Obesity* 2 (3): 153–58.

AAP (American Academy of Pediatrics), APHA (American Public Health Association) & NRC (National Resource Center for Health and Safety in Child Care and Early Education). 2002. *Caring for our children: National health and safety performance standards: Guidelines for out-of-home child care programs.* 2d ed. Elk Grove Village, IL: American Academy of Pediatrics; Washington, DC: American Public Health Association.

Ballard, K., D. Caldwell, C. Dunn, A. Hardison, J. Newkirk, M. Sanderson, S. Thaxton Vodicka & C. Thomas. 2005. *Move more: NC's recommended standards for physical activity in school.* Raleigh, NC: North Carolina DHHS, NC Division of Public Health.

Barros, R.M., E.J. Silver & R.E.K. Stein. 2009. School recess and group classroom behavior. *Pediatrics* 123 (2): 431–36.

Benenson, J.F., H.P. Carder & S.J. Geib-Cole. 2008. The development of boys' preferential pleasure in physical aggression. *Aggressive Behavior* 34 (2): 154–66.

Bjorklund, D.F., & R.D. Brown. 1998. Physical play and cognitive development: Integrating activity, cognition, and education. *Child Development* 69 (3): 604–06.

Bjorklund, D., & A. Pellegrini. 2001. *The origins of human nature.* Washington, DC: American Psychological Association.

Boulton, M.J. 1993. A comparison of adults' and children's abilities to distinguish between aggressive and playful fighting in middle school pupils: Implications for playground supervision and behavior management. *Educational Studies* 19 (3): 193–204.

Boulton, M.J. 1996. A comparison of 8- and 11-year-old girls' and boys' participation in specific types of rough-and-tumble play and aggressive fighting: Implications for functional hypotheses. *Aggressive Behavior* 22 (4): 271–87.

Boulton, M., & P.K. Smith. 1992. The social nature of play fighting and play chasing: Mechanisms and strategies underlying cooperation and compromise. In *The adapted mind: Evolutionary psychology and the generation of culture*, eds. J.H. Barkow, L. Cosmides & J. Tooby, 429–44. New York: Oxford University Press.

Bower, J.K., D.P. Hales, D.F. Tate, D.A. Rubin, S.E. Benjamin & D.S. Ward. 2008. The childcare environment and children's physical activity. *American Journal of Preventive Medicine* 34 (1): 23–29.

Boyd, D., & H. Bee. 2006. *Lifespan development.* 4th ed. Boston: Pearson.

Bredekamp, S., ed. 1987. *Developmentally appropriate practice in early childhood programs serving children from birth through 8.* Expanded ed. Washington, DC: NAEYC.

Bredekamp, S., & C. Copple, eds. 1997. *Developmentally appropriate practice in early childhood programs.* Rev. ed. Washington, DC: NAEYC.

Brownell, C.A., S. Zerwas & G.B. Ramani. 2007. "So big": The development of body self-awareness in toddlers. *Child Development* 78 (5): 1426–40.

Burdette, H.L., & R.C. Whitaker. 2005. Resurrecting free play in young children: Looking beyond fitness and fatness to attention, affiliation, and affect. *Archives of Pediatrics & Adolescent Medicine* 159 (1): 46–50.

Byers, J.A. 1998. The biology of human play. *Child Development* 69 (3): 599–600.

Byrd-Williams, C., L.A. Kelly, J.N. Davis, D. Spruitz-Metz & M.I. Goran. 2007. Influence of gender, BMI, and Hispanic ethnicity on physical activity in children. *International Journal of Pediatric Obesity* 2 (3): 159–66.

Cardon, G., E. Van Cauwenberghe, V. Labarque, L. Haerens & I. De Bourdeaudhuij. 2008. The contributions of preschool playground factors in explaining children's physical activity during recess. *International Journal of Behavioral Nutrition and Physical Activity* 5 (11): 1186–92.

Carlson, F.M. 2006. *Essential touch: Meeting the needs of young children.* Washington, DC: NAEYC.

Carlson, F.M. 2009. Rough & tumble play 101. *Child Care Information Exchange* 31 (4): 70–73.

Carson, J., V. Burks & R. Parke. 1993. Parent-child physical play: Determinants and consequences. In *Parent-child play*, ed. K. MacDonald, 197–220. Albany: State University of New York Press.

Case-Smith, J., & H.M. Kuhaneck. 2008. Play preferences of typically developing children and children with developmental delays between ages 3 and 7 years. *Occupational Therapy Journal of Research* 28 (1): 19–29.

Cashmore, A.W., & S.C. Jones. 2008. Growing up active: A study into physical activity in long day care centers. *Journal of Research in Childhood Education* 23 (2): 179–91.

Coe, D.P., J.M. Pivarnik, C.J. Womack, M.J. Reeves & R.M. Malina. 2006. Effect of physical education and activity levels on academic achievement in children. *Medicine & Science in Sports & Exercise* 38 (8): 1515–19.

Connor, J. M., & L.A. Serbin. 1977. Behaviorally based masculine- and feminine-activity-preference scales for preschoolers: Correlates with other classroom behaviors and cognitive tests. *Child Development* 48 (4): 1411–16.

Copple, C., & S. Bredekamp, eds. 2009. *Developmentally appropriate practice in early childhood programs serving children from birth through 8*. 3d ed. Washington, DC: NAEYC.

CPSC (U.S. Consumer Product Safety Commission). *Public playground safety checklist*. CPSC Document #327. Online: www.cpsc.gov/cpscpub/pubs/327.html.

Curtis, D. 2010. What's the risk of no risk? *Child Care Information Exchange* 32 (2): 52–56.

Curtis, D., & M. Carter. 2005. Rethinking early childhood environments to enhance learning. *Young Children* 60 (3): 34–38.

Csikszentmihalyi, M. 1981. Some paradoxes in the definition of play. In *Play as context*, ed. A.T. Cheska, 14–26. West Point, NY: Leisure Press.

DeCorby, K., J. Halas, S. Dixon, I. Wintrup & H. Janzen. 2005. Classroom teachers and the challenges of delivering quality physical education. *Journal of Educational Research* 98 (4): 208–20.

Diamond, A. 2000. Close interrelation of motor development and cognitive development and of the cerebellum and prefontal cortex. *Child Development* 71 (1): 44–56.

DiPietro, J.A. 1981. Rough and tumble play: A function of gender. *Developmental Psychology* 17 (1): 50–58.

Dowda, M., R. Pate, S.G. Trost, M.J. Almeida & J.R. Sirard. 2004. Influences of preschool policies and practices on children's physical activity. *Journal of Community Health* 29 (3): 183–96.

Fabes, R.A. 1994. Physiological, emotional, and behavioral correlates of gender segregation. In *Childhood gender segregation: Causes and consequences*, ed. C. Leaper, 19–34. San Francisco: Jossey-Bass.

Farrington, D.P. 2005. Childhood origins of antisocial behavior. *Clinical Psychology and Psychotherapy* 12 (3): 177–90.

Finn, K., N. Johannsen & B. Specker. 2002. Factors associated with physical activity in preschool children. *The Journal of Pediatrics* 140 (1): 81–85.

Flanders, J.L., V. Leo, D. Paquette, R.O. Pihl & J.R. Seguin. 2009. Rough-and-tumble play and regulation of aggression: An observational study of father-child play dyads. *Aggressive Behavior* 35 (4): 285–95.

Fromberg, D.P., & D.F. Gullo. 1992. Perspectives on children. In *Encyclopedia of early childhood education*, eds. L.R. Williams & D.P. Fromberg, 191–94. New York: Garland Publishing.

Fry, D. 1987. Differences between play fighting and serious fighting among Zapotec children. *Ethology and Sociobiology* 8 (4): 285–306.

Fry, D. 1990. Play aggression among Zapotec children: Implications for the practice hypothesis. *Aggressive Behavior* 16 (5): 321–40.

Fry, D. 2005. Rough-and-tumble social play in humans. In *The nature of play: Great apes and humans*, eds. A.D. Pellegrini & P.K. Smith, 54–85. New York: Guilford Press.

Gabbard, C.P. 2007. *Lifelong motor development.* 5th ed. Boston: Allyn & Bacon.

Gallahue, D.I. 1995. Transforming physical education curriculum. In *Reaching potentials, volume 2: Transforming early childhood curriculum and assessment,* eds. S. Bredekamp & T. Rosegrant, 125–44. Washington, DC: NAEYC.

Garvey, C. 1977. *Play.* Cambridge, MA: Harvard University Press.

Georgia Department of Early Care and Learning. n.d. *Georgia early learning standards: Infants.* Online: http://decal.ga.gov/documents/attachments/GELSSection3.pdf.

Georgia Department of Early Care and Learning. 2011. *Rules for child care learning centers.* Online: http://decal.ga.gov/documents/attachments/CCLCRulesandRegulations.pdf.

Greenman, J. 2007. *Caring spaces, learning places: Children's environments that work.* Redmond, WA: Exchange Press.

Greenman, J.A., A. Stonehouse & G. Schweikert. 2008. *Prime times: A handbook for excellence in infant and toddler programs.* St. Paul, MN: Redleaf Press.

Grissom, J.B. 2005. Physical fitness and academic achievement. *Journal of Exercise Physiology* 8 (1): 11–25.

Groos, K. 1901. *The play of man.* London: William Heinemann.

Hartup, W.W. 1983. Peer relations. In *Handbook of child psychology, volume 4: Socialization, personality, and social development*, eds. E. M. Hetherington & P.H. Mussen, 103–96. New York: Wiley.

Hellendoorn, J., & J.H.F. Harinck. 1997. War toy play and aggression in Dutch kindergarten children. *Social Development* 6 (3): 340–54.

Hessler, K.L. Physical activity behaviors of rural preschoolers. *Practice Applications of Research* 35 (4): 246–53.

Hillman, C.H., D.M. Casteili & S.M. Buck. 2005. Aerobic fitness and neurocognitive function in healthy preadolescent children. *Medicine & Science in Sports & Exercise* 37 (11): 1967–74.

Hines, M., S. Golombok, J. Rust, K. Johnston & J. Golding. 2002. Testosterone during pregnancy and gender role behaviour of pre-school children: A longitudinal population study. *Child Development* 73 (6): 1678–87.

Holland, P. 2003. *We don't play with guns here: War, weapon, and superhero play in the early years.* Maidenhead, England: Open University Press.

Honig, A.S. 2009. Early discoveries. *Scholastic Parent & Child* 17 (2): 90.

Houck, G.M. 1999. The measurement of child characteristics from infancy to toddlerhood: Temperament, developmental competence, self-concept, and social competence. *Issues in Comprehensive Pediatric Nursing* 22 (2/3): 101–27.

Houck, G.M., & A.M. Spegman. 1999. The development of self: Theoretical understanding and conceptual underpinnings. *Infants & Young Children* 12 (1): 1–16.

Humphreys, A.P., & P.K. Smith. 1984. Rough-and-tumble play in preschool and playground. In *Play in animals and humans*, ed. P. K. Smith, 241–70. Oxford: Blackwell.

Humphreys, A.P., & P.K. Smith. 1987. Rough and tumble, friendships, and dominance in schoolchildren: Evidence for continuity and change with age. *Child Development* 58 (1): 201–12.

Illinois Department of Children and Family Services. 2010. *Licensing standards for day care centers.* Online: www.state.il.us/dcfs/docs/407.pdf.

Jarvis, P. 2007a. Dangerous activities within an invisible playground: A study of emergent male football play and teachers' perspectives of outdoor free play in the early years of primary school. *International Journal of Early Years Education* 15 (3): 245–59.

Jarvis, P. 2007b. Monsters, magic and Mr. Psycho: A biocultural approach to rough and tumble play in the early years of primary school. *Early Years* 27 (2): 171–88.

Jordan, E. 1995. Fighting boys and fantasy play: The construction of masculinity in the early years of school. *Gender and Education* 7 (1): 69–87.

Keyser, J. 2006. *From parents to partners: Building a family-centered early childhood program.* St. Paul, MN: Redleaf Press; Washington, DC: NAEYC.

KidsHealth. 2008. *Playground safety.* Online: http://kidshealth.org/parents/firstaid_safe/outdoor/playground.html.

Light, S.N., J.A. Coan, C. Zahn-Waxler, C. Frye, H.H. Goldsmith & R.J. Davidson. 2009. Empathy is associated with dynamic change in prefrontal brain electrical activity during positive emotion in children. *Child Development* 80 (4): 1210–31.

Litmanovitz, I., T. Dolfin, O. Friedland, S. Arnon, R. Regev, R. Shainkin-Kestenbaum, M. Lis & A. Eliakim. 2003. Early physical activity intervention prevents decrease of bone strength in very low birth weight infants. *Pediatrics* 112 (1): 15–19.

Little, H. 2006. Children's risk-taking behavior: Implications for early childhood policy and practice. *International Journal of Early Years Education* 14 (2): 141–54.

Lofdahl, A. 2005. Preschool teachers' conceptions of children's "chaotic play." In *Play: An interdisciplinary synthesis*, eds. F.F. McMahon, D.E. Lytle & B. Sutton-Smith, 195–204. Lanham, MD: University Press of America.

Logue, M.E., & H. Harvey. 2010. Preschool teachers' views of active play. *Journal of Research in Childhood Education* 24 (1): 32–49.

Malloy, H.L., & P. McMurray-Schwarz. 2004. War play, aggression and peer culture: A review of the research examining the relationship between war play and aggression. In *Advances in early education and day care, volume 13: Social contexts of early education, and reconceptualizing play (II)*, eds. S. Reifel & M. Brown, 235–65. Bingley, UK: Emerald Group Publishing Limited.

McClelland, M.M., A.C. Acock & F.J. Morrison. 2006. The impact of kindergarten learning-related skills on academic trajectories at the end of elementary school. *Early Childhood Research Quarterly* 21 (4): 471–90.

McCune, L. 1998. Immediate and ultimate functions of physical activity play. *Child Development* 69 (3): 601–03.

McEvoy, M.A., T.L. Estrem, M.C. Rodriguez & M.L. Olson. 2003. Assessing relational and physical aggression among preschool children. *Topics in Early Childhood Special Education* 23 (2): 53–63.

Mitchell, R., M. Cavanagh & D. Eagers. 2006. Not all risk is bad: Playgrounds as a learning environment. *International Journal of Injury Control and Safety Promotion* 13 (2): 122–24.

Meany, M., J. Stewart & W.W. Beatty. 1985. Sex differences in social play. In *Advances in the study of behavior*, eds. J. Rosenblatt, C. Beer, M.C. Bushnel & P. Slater, 2–58. New York: Academic Press.

Morrongiello, B.A. 2005. Caregiver supervision and child-injury risk: I. Issues in defining and measuring supervision; II. Findings and direction for future research. *Journal of Pediatric Psychology* 30 (7): 536–52.

NAEYC (National Association for the Education of Young Children). 2005. *Physical environment: A guide to the NAEYC Early Childhood Program Standard and related Accreditation Criteria*. Washington, DC: Author.

NASPE (National Association for Sport and Physical Education). 2004. *Physical activity for children: A statement of guidelines for children ages 5–12*. 2d ed. Reston, VA: Author.

NASPE (National Association for Sport and Physical Education). 2009a. *Active start: A statement of physical activity guidelines for children from birth to age 5*. 2d ed. Reston, VA: Author. Online: www.aahperd.org/naspe/standards/nationalGuidelines/ActiveStart.cfm.

NASPE (National Association for Sport and Physical Education). 2009b. *Appropriate maximum class length for elementary physical education*. Position statement. Reston, VA: Author.

New York State Office of Children & Family Services. 2010. *Family day care provider handbook*. Online: http://ocfs.ny.gov/main/publications/Pub4623.pdf.

O'Donnell, M., & S. Sharpe. 2004. The social construction of youthful masculinities: Peer group sub-cultures. In *RoutledgeFalmer reader in sociology of education*, ed. S. Ball, 89–127. London: RoutledgeFalmer.

Olsen, H., D. Thompson & S. Hudson. 2011. Outdoor learning: Supervision is more than watching children play. *Dimensions of Early Childhood* 39 (1): 3–9.

Ostrov, J.M., & C.F. Keating. 2004. Gender differences in preschool aggression during free play and structured interactions: An observational study. *Social Development* 13 (2): 255–77.

Paquette, D., R. Carbonneau, D. Dubeau, M. Bigras & R.E. Tremblay. 2003. Prevalence of father-child rough-and-tumble play and physical aggression in preschool children. *European Journal of Psychology of Education* 18 (2): 171–89.

Paley, V.G. 1992. *You can't say you can't play*. Cambridge, MA: Harvard University Press.

Pellegrini, A.D. 1987. Rough-and-tumble play: Developmental and educational significance. *Educational Psychology* 22 (11): 23–43.

Pellegrini, A.D. 1989. Categorising children's rough and tumble play. *Play and Culture* 2 (1): 48–51.

Pellegrini, A.D. 1995. *School recess and playground behavior: Educational and developmental roles.* Albany, NY: State University of New York Press.

Pellegrini, A.D. 2002. Perceptions of playfighting and real fighting: Effects of sex and participant status. In *Conceptual, social-cognitive, and contextual issues in the field of play*, ed. J. Roopnarine, 223–33. Westport, CT: Albex Publishing.

Pellegrini, A.D. 2003. Perceptions and functions of play and real fighting in early adolescence. *Child Development* 74 (5): 1522–33.

Pellegrini, A.D., & P. Blatchford. 2000. *The child at school.* London: Arnold.

Pellegrini, A.D., & J.C. Perlmutter. 1988. The diagnostic and therapeutic roles of children's rough-and-tumble play. *Children's Health Care* 16 (3): 162–68.

Pellegrini, A.D., & P.K. Smith. 1998a. Physical activity play: Consensus and debate. *Child Development* 69 (3): 609–10.

Pellegrini, A.D., & P.K. Smith. 1998b. Physical activity play: The nature and function of a neglected aspect of play. *Child Development* 69 (3): 577–98.

Pellis, S.M., E.F. Field, L.K. Smith & V.C. Pellis. 1996. Multiple differences in the play fighting of male and female rats. *Neuroscience and Biobehavioral Reviews* 21 (1): 105–20.

Pellis, S.M., E.F. Field & I.Q. Whishaw. 1999. The development of a sex-differentiated defensive motor pattern in rats: A possible role for juvenile experience. *Developmental Psychobiology* 35: 156–64.

Pellis, S.M., & V.C. Pellis. 2007. Rough-and-tumble play and the development of the social brain. *Association of Psychological Science* 16 (2): 95–98.

Peterson, L., B. Ewigman & C. Kivlahan. 1993. Judgments regarding appropriate child supervision to prevent injury: The role of environmental risk and child age. *Child Development* 64: 934–50.

Pica, R. 2006. *A running start: How play, physical activity and free time create a successful child.* New York: Marlowe & Company.

Porter, R. 1994. Roughhousing as a style of play. *Child Care Information Exchange* 17 (3): 44–45.

Prellwitz, M., & L. Skar. 2007. Usability of playgrounds for children with different abilities. *Occupational Therapy International* 14 (3): 144–55.

Reed, T.L. 2005. A qualitative approach to boys' rough and tumble play: There is more than meets the eye. In *Play: An interdisciplinary synthesis*, eds. F.F. McMahon, D.E. Lytle & B. Sutton-Smith, 53–71. Lanham, MD: University Press of America.

Reed, T., & M. Brown. 2000. The expression of care in the rough and tumble play of boys. *Journal of Research in Childhood Education* 15 (1): 104–16.

Robertson, M.A. 1984. Changing motor patterns during childhood. In *Motor development during childhood and adolescence,* ed. J.R. Thomas, 48–90. Minneapolis, MN: Burgess.

Rosin, H. 2010. The end of men. *The Atlantic*, July/August 2010. Online: www.theatlantic.com/magazine/archive/2010/07/the-end-of-men/8135.

Rough and tumble play. October 28, 2008. Video, 10:00. Online: www.tvo.org/TVO/WebObjects/TVO.woa?videoid?24569407001.

Sandberg, A., & I. Pramling-Samuelsson. 2005. An interview study of gender differences in preschool teachers' attitudes toward children's play. *Early Childhood Education Journal* 32 (5): 297–305.

Sanders, S.W. 2002. *Active for life: Developmentally appropriate movement programs for young children.* Washington, DC: NAEYC.

Sanders, S.W. 2006. Physical education in kindergarten. In *K today: Teaching and learning in the kindergarten year,* ed. D.F. Gullo, 85–94. Washington, DC: NAEYC.

Scales, B., M. Almy, A. Nicolopulou & S. Ervin-Tripp. 1991. Defending play in the lives of children. In *Play and the social context of development in early care and education*, eds. B. Scales, M. Almy, A. Nicolopulou & S. Ervin-Tripp, 15–31. New York: Teachers College Press.

Schafer, M., & P.K. Smith. 1996. Teachers' perceptions of play fighting and real fighting in primary school. *Educational Research* 38 (2): 173–81.

Scott, E., & J. Panksepp. 2003. Rough-and-tumble play in human children. *Aggressive Behavior* 29 (6): 539–51.

Shannon, J.D., C.S. Tamis-LeMonda, K. London & N. Cabrera. 2002. Beyond rough and tumble: Low-income fathers' interactions and children's cognitive development at 24 months. *Parenting: Science and Practice* 2 (2): 77–104.

Sheets-Johnstone, M. 2008. *The roots of morality.* University Park, PA: The Pennsylvania State University Press.

Shephard, R.J. 1996. Habitual physical activity and academic performance. *Nutrition Reviews* 54 (4): 32–36.

Silverman, I., & M. Eals. 1992. Sex differences in spatial ability: Evolutionary theory and data. In *The adapted mind: Evolutionary psychology and the generation of culture*, eds. H. Barkow, L. Cosmides & J. Tooby, 533–49. New York: Oxford University Press.

Singer, D.G., R. Michnik Golinkoff & K. Hirsh-Pasek, eds. 2006. *Play=learning: How play motivates and enhances children's cognitive and social-emotional growth.* New York: Oxford University Press.

Smith, P.K., R., Smees & A.D. Pellegrini. 2004. Play fighting and real fighting: Using video playback methodology with young children. *Aggressive Behavior* 30: 164–73.

Smith, P.K., R. Smees, A.D. Pellegrini & E. Menesini. 2002. Comparing pupil and teacher perceptions for playful fighting, serious fighting, and positive peer interaction. In *Conceptual, social-cognitive, and contextual issues in the field of play*, ed. J. Roopnarine, 235–45. Westport, CT: Albex Publishing.

Sola, K., N. Brekke & M. Brekke. 2010. An activity-based intervention for obese and physically inactive children organized in primary care: Feasibility and impact on fitness and BMI. *Scandinavian Journal of Primary Health Care* 28 (4): 199–204.

Starfield, B. 1992. Child and adolescent health status measures. *The Future of Children* 2 (2): 25–39. A publication of the Center for the Future of Children, The David and Lucile Packard Foundation.

Stephenson, A. 2003. Physical risk-taking: Dangerous or endangered? *Early Years* 23 (1): 35–43.

Stevens, T.A., Y. To, S.J. Stevenson & M.R. Lochbaum. 2008. The importance of physical activity and physical education in the prediction of academic achievement. *Journal of Sports Behavior* 31 (4): 368–88.

Stolzer, J.M. 2008. Boys and the American education system: A biocultural review of the literature. *Ethical Human Psychology and Psychiatry* 10 (2): 80–95.

Strayer, F.F. 1980. Social ecology of the preschool peer group. In *The Minnesota Symposia on Child Development, volume 13. Development of cognition, affect, and social relationships*, ed. W.A. Collins, 165–96. Hillsdale, NJ: Erlbaum.

Tamis-LeMonda, C.S. 2004. Conceptualizing fathers' roles: Playmates and more. *Human Development* 47 (4): 220–27.

Tannock, M. 2008. Rough and tumble play: An investigation of the perceptions of educators and young children. *Early Childhood Education Journal* 35 (4): 357–61.

Taras, H. 2005. Physical activity and student performance at school. *Journal of School Health* 75 (6): 214–18.

Texas Department of Family and Protective Services. 2010. *Minimum standard rules for licensed child-care centers*. Online: www.dfps.state.tx.us/documents/ Child_Care/pdf/746_weighted-formatted-pg_adopted_12-10_rules.pdf.

Thelen, E., & L.B. Smith. 1998. Dynamic systems theories. In *Handbook of child psychology, volume 1: Theoretical models of human development, 5th ed.,* ed. R.M. Lerner, 563–634. New York: John Wiley & Sons.

Thompson, R.A. 2001. Development in the first years of life. *The Future of Children* 11 (1): 21–33.

Tomporowski, P.D., C.L. Davis, P.H. Miller & J.A. Naglieri. 2008. Exercise and children's intelligence, cognition, and academic achievement. *Educational Psychology Review* 20 (2): 111–31.

Trawick-Smith, J. 2006. *Early childhood development: A multicultural perspective, 4th ed.* Upper Saddle River, NJ: Merrill.

Uchiyama, I., J.J. Campos, C.B. Frankel, D.L. Anderson, D. Witherington, L. Lejeune & M. Barbu-Roth. 2008. Locomotor experience affects self and emotion. *Developmental Psychology* 44 (5): 1225–31.

Vaughn, B.E., & E. Waters. 1981. Attention structure, sociometric status, and dominance: Interrelations, behavioral correlates, and relationships to social competence. *Developmental Psychology* 17 (3): 275–88.

Vestal, A., & N.A. Jones. 2004. Peace building and conflict resolution in preschool children. *Journal of Research in Childhood Education* 19 (2): 131–42.

Ward, D.S. 2010. Physical activity in young children: The role of child care. *Medicine & Science in Sports & Exercise* 42 (3): 499–501.